FOUR EGYPTIAN
MARTYRS

SAINT **SHENOUDA** PRESS

FOUR EGYPTIAN
MARTYRS

Translated by
Fr Robert J Nixon

ST SHENOUDA PRESS
SYDNEY, AUSTRALIA

2021

Four Egyptian Martyrs
Translated by: Fr Robert J Nixon

COPYRIGHT © 2021
St. Shenouda Press

ST SHENOUDA PRESS
8419 Putty Rd,
Putty, NSW, 2330
Sydney, Australia

www.stshenoudapress.com

ISBN 13: 978-0-6451394-4-0

Cover Design:
Dionysia Tanios
@dionysiandesigns

Contents

TRANSLATOR'S INTRODUCTION

Strength and endurance together form the noble and
illustrious pair of virtues that most aptly befits, adorns
and distinguishes all the saints.[1]
St. Cyril of Alexandria

In the early fourth century, under the reign of the emperor
Diocletian, followers of the Christian Faith experienced a
sustained and systematic campaign of fierce persecution at the
hands of the Roman authorities. The aim of this persecution
was nothing less than the entire abolition of the true Faith and
the utter destruction of the Church. Much blood was shed
and many lives were lost for the holy Name of Christ. And the
threat made to Christians was not simply death alone. Tortures
of horrendous cruelty were devised and employed in a manner
which seems to exceed the boundaries of human possibility.
Whilst these persecutions were conducted throughout the
entire Roman empire, they were particularly vitriolic and savage
in Egypt. An immense number of Egyptian Christians of the
period received the noble crown of martyrdom, responding
to the cruelty and inhumanity of their persecutors with a

---

1 St. Cyril of Alexandria, "Oratiuncula I, in Translatione Reliquiarum SS.
Martyrum Cyri et Joannis", PG 77:1100.

heroism and fidelity which remains profoundly astonishing and wondrously inspiring.

This volume presents in English translation (mostly for the first time) ancient Coptic versions of the lives of four Egyptian martyrs who each died under the reign of Diocletian. These are St. Epime of Pancoleus, St. Abanoub of Nehisa. St. Apatil of Sabaru and St. Lacaron of Tgeliensis. Each of these were youths or young men who faced a range of appalling and often bizarre tortures with exemplary courage and fortitude, before accepting final martyrdom at the hands of the imperial authorities.

There are conspicuous overlaps of historical details and personages in their respective stories. Two of the lives (those of St. Epime and St. Abanoub) are written by the same author, St. Julius of Aqfas, who was an eye witness to many of the events he describes. This Julius, who had served as an official scribe to the court in Alexandria, was himself destined to end his life as a martyr. The same historical personages—notably Armenius, a ruler or prince of Alexandria, and Arius, a provincial governor—re-appear in most of the lives. These elements of historical consistency and overlapping of characters and events contribute to establishing the reliability and coherence of the histories, when viewed as a total corpus.

Diocletian held the imperial throne from 284 to 305 AD. Yet he was neither the sole monarch nor uncontested head of the Empire throughout most of this time. He was not born of royal or even aristocratic blood, but rose through the ranks of the army to the very highest circles of power. He was proclaimed emperor in 284 AD by popular acclamation of the military. Yet Carinus, the surviving son of the former emperor Carus, had an apparently valid claim both of heredity and law, that the imperial dignity rightly belonged to him rather than Diocletian. Indeed, he was, at least initially, recognized as the legitimate emperor by most of the civil authorities in Rome. With these (and other) rival claimants to the throne, the political situation was gravely uncertain, to say the least.

In 286 AD a certain general, Maximian, was appointed co-emperor by Diocletian, for reasons which are not entirely clear. He seems, in due course, also to have become a rival claimant to the imperial dignity. There are, as may be expected, many conflicting narratives and perspectives offered from various sources on the issue of the relationship between Diocletian and Maximian. Yet it is evident that Diocletian himself was an unstable, vicious and ruthless character; and that Maximian was no less determined or cruel in his persecution of the Christians than the principal emperor. Indeed, the campaign referred to as the 'Diocletian persecution' continued for some years after the voluntary abdication of Diocletian himself in 305. The persecution did not end officially until 311, a year before the conversion of Constantine the Great in 312 AD.

It is pertinent to note that persecutions of Christians had been only intermittent under the Roman Empire prior to its adoption of Christianity as the official state religion. Indeed, in most cases, the imperial authorities preferred to maintain an attitude of indifferent tolerance towards diverse faiths and cultic practices—something which was undoubtedly a judicious practical expedient, given the ethnically and culturally heterogenous nature of the Empire. Many localized cults abounded in the diverse corners of the realm; but evidently the followers of such cults did not generally consider it incongruous to make sacrifices also to the official Roman gods while continuing to believe in and worship their own local deities.

Yet for Christians—who believe in One God only—to 'compromise' and make sacrifice to the official gods was necessarily an unacceptable thing to do. The refusal of the

Christians to carry out the required sacrifices to the official gods was thus the critical issue. This is evident in many instances in the lives contained in this volume, in which a governor urges the saint to 'compromise', not requiring him to believe sincerely in the Roman gods but merely to follow the customary official ceremonial observances and to refrain from espousing Christianity openly.

Apart from the details of the Diocletian persecution which can be gleaned from the individual narratives and histories of the martyrs who died under that emperor, a reliable synoptic recounting of the campaign is to be found in the *Church Histories* of Eusebius of Caesarea. The details given by Eusebius (who was a contemporary and witness to the persecution) accord closely with the state of affairs exhibited in the descriptions of the individual martyrdoms contained herein. According to Eusebius, the persecution commenced in the nineteenth year of the reign of Diocletian, that is, approximately 303 AD. At that time:

> *(..) An imperial decree was promulgated everywhere, demanding that churches be razed to the ground and that Scriptures be destroyed by fire; and notifying that those in positions of honor would lose their reputation, and that freeborn citizens, if they continued in the Christian faith, would be deprived of their liberty. Certainly, such was the initial edict against us. But not much later other decrees arrived, ordering that all bishops of the churches everywhere should be put in chains, and then compelled to offer sacrifice by every means of coercion possible.*[2]

---

2 Eusebius of Caesarea, "Historiae Ecclesiasticiae" VIII.2, PG XX:746-747.

This description of Eusebius matches very closely with that found at the beginning of the lives of most of the martyrs contained in the present volume. The lives of St. Epime, St. Abanoub and St. Apatil all, in fact, quote directly the edict of persecution issued by Diocletian. While these reproductions of the edict do not coincide in their exact wording, the effect and sense of each is identical, and, in turn, accords precisely with that given by Eusebius.

At the beginning of the life of St. Epime, the author, St. Julius of Aqfas—who was both a contemporary and, as an imperial scribe, confidently entrusted with the secrets of the highest circles—provides a more elaborate account, which is striking, colorful and very plausible in its details (not found elsewhere) of the reasons for, and the circumstances of, Diocletian's resolve to persecute the Christians. He writes:

> *It happened that during the reign of the emperor Diocletian, that wicked and sinful tyrant, that the devil caused his heart to stray from the One God of Heaven. This happened initially because of a crime committed by a certain archbishop by the name of Gaius, who—having been bribed—had secretly released from prison Nicodemus, the son of Sapor, the king of Persia. And then, with lying oaths, and to conceal his unlawful actions, Gaius had told the story that this Nicodemus [whose true whereabouts were unknown to all] had, in fact, died.*

> *When the emperor heard of this dishonesty on the part of Gaius, he ordered that burning asphalt and pitch should be poured down the throat of this archbishop, until he was dead. And after this,*

now filled with antipathy and disbelief towards the true God of Christianity and all adherents of the Christian religion, Diocletian gathered a vast treasury of pure gold, and had seventy statues fashioned from it. These statues he declared to be gods. The largest and most splendid he called Apollo—and the others he identified as Jupiter, Serapis, Athena, Artemis, and the various other deities of the pagan pantheon.

And Diocletian gathered all his nobles and leading officials to himself, saying: "Listen to me, my friends, for I wish to speak to you all!" They replied, "Please speak to us, O lord and King!"

And he said to them, (…). "Last night, as I lay down to sleep, it happened that the great god Apollo came to me, and all the other gods following him. And they spoke to me, saying, 'Behold, we have made you strong! We have given you victory in battle. Now you, in return, should glorify us throughout your empire.' So, my friends, what should I do, in order to fulfil this instruction from the gods?"

A certain general, Romanus, (…) said to the emperor, "Hear me, O King, and I shall advise you. (…) Arise and write an edict to all the people of Egypt, and send it to each of the cities and towns (…) You should order that all churches consecrated to the name of Christ be destroyed, and that temples for the worship of the Roman gods should be constructed instead in every city and village. And command that your troops should assemble all Christian priests, deacons and lectors—together with all the leading city officials—and instruct them that it is absolutely forbidden to offer worship, praise or sacrifice to the Name of Christ. And let them burn with fire every book of Sacred Scripture or of Christian doctrine which they can find!"

Now this proposal was most pleasing to emperor Diocletian, who exclaimed, "Through the great god Apollo, let it be done as you have suggested!" He then pronounced a promulgation to this effect against all Christians. Rising early the next morning, which was the first day of the month of Parmouti,[3] he wrote the following decree: "I, Diocletian the Emperor, write to all my kingdom; and the following orders are issued to all who are subject to my command, whether officers, soldiers or civilians. Let the Name of Jesus not be found in the mouth of anyone, and let all worship and make sacrifice to the great gods of Rome." And thus it was done.

Eusebius makes specific comments on the Egyptian martyrs of this time, noting in particular the atrocious nature of the tortures to which they were subjected, and their courage and fortitude in the face of these:

---

3 April 9.

Did anyone ever see (the sufferings of the Egyptian martyrs) without being filled with admiration at the innumerable scourgings and the endurance displayed under them by these truly illustrious athletes of the Christian Faith; at the battle against savage beasts who were accustomed to licking blood, when they were attacked by panthers, by immense bears, by wild boars and by bulls incited to fury with red-hot irons; at the admirable endurance of these most strong martyrs against every type of beast? (…)

Miraculous indeed was the bold constancy of these saints, and the unflinching and stable fortitude of soul which resided within their tender bodies. You could see a youth barely twenty years of age, standing without chains, spreading out his arms in the form of a cross, and praying to God with a firm and unwavering soul; and not retreating from where he stood, though bears and panthers breathing fury and death were about to seize his limbs with their bits. Yet by some Divine power—I cannot say what—their mouths were stopped, and they ran back again to the rear. Again, you would have seen others—there were five altogether—cast to a raging bull. When others approached from outside, the bull tossed them with his horns into the air and mangled them leaving them to be collected, almost dead; but when, in fury, it rushed head-

down at the lonely group of holy martyrs it could not even get near them! It stamped its feet and pushed with its horns in all directions. Goaded on by the fiery irons, it breathed forth rage and threats, but Divine providence held it back from the attack. So, as the bulls did their intended victims no harm whatever, other beasts were set upon them. At last, after these animals had launched their gruesome and varied assaults, the martyrs were one and all thrust through with the sword, and instead of being buried in the earth were committed to the waves of the sea. [4]

(Throughout Egypt, there were) immense numbers of men, together with their wives and children, who were contemptuous of this passing and ephemeral life, and who faced death in all its forms for the sake of our Savior's teaching. Some were flayed, stretched, mercilessly flogged, subjected to countless other torments, too cruel and terrible to describe, in an endless variety, and finally given over to the flames; some were submerged in the sea; others readily stretched out their necks to accept the executioner's axe; some died under torture; others were starved to death; again others were crucified, some in the way that villains customarily are, but some with still greater cruelty were nailed upside down, head down, and preserved alive until

---

4 Eusebius of Caesarea, "Historiae Ecclesiasticiae" VIII.7, PG XX:755-758.

they perished from lack of food, upon the gallows themselves. [5]

The description of the varied types of tortures inflicted upon the Egyptian martyrs is reflected in fuller and more detailed form in the lives of the individual saints which follow. Indeed, many readers will find these descriptions both terrifying and appalling. But the accurate and honest description of such things is one of the primary literary features of these Coptic hagiographies. If the descriptions of the acts of the martyrs from the same period written by Latin authors perhaps tend to pass over such things somewhat restrainedly or to describe them only in broad and general terms, such was most emphatically not the case for the Coptic authors. Of course, to describe the tortures which these saints faced in accurate, vivid and 'unsoftened' terms—while occasionally uncomfortable, perhaps, for the sensitive reader—serves to illustrate their courage and endurance all the more powerfully.

Throughout the acts of the martyrs presented here, a number of common literary and narrative *motifs* are readily identified. The prevalence of these common elements both define and constitute these writings as a literary genre; but, at the same time, they reflect a historical reality which was the common experience of many martyrs during those years. Five such *motifs* are enumerated below, with comments on and illustrations of each.

Motif I: The protagonist (that is, the saint himself) is a male youth or a very young man, and of handsome appearance.

In each of the lives included here, the saint is a boy or male youth, or a very young man. The most notable case of this youthfulness is St. Abanoub, who was merely twelve years old

---

5 Eusebius of Caesarea, "Historiae Ecclesiasticiae" VIII.8, PG XX:757-761.

at the time of his martyrdom. The age of St. Lacaron is given as fourteen years, and that of St. Apatil as sixteen years. The exact age of St. Epime is not stated, but he is described as a young man and still living in his parents' house. Yet Lacaron and Apatil were both already soldiers, and Epime was evidently respected as a leader among the Christians of his village. Of course, notions of the development of maturity are, to some degree, socially conditioned. Whereas in most modern cultures, a male of fourteen years would be viewed as a child, in much of the ancient world, including fourth century Egypt, such a person would often have been considered a young adult. Indeed, when facing their trials and persecutions, it is clear that each of them (including twelve-year old Abanoub) were assumed to be fully responsible and accountable for their own independent actions. Moreover, comment is made on the handsome appearance of each of the saints. This is perhaps not surprising in the context of the widespread and almost universal literary convention (which seems to be common to virtually all times and cultures) of portraying heroes and heroines as being of attractive appearance. Yet this attractive appearance is most appropriately understood as being not merely a question of physical features or proportions, but emanating from and reflecting nobility and purity of moral character, manner and disposition. As well as being valuable historical documents for future generations, the narratives of these martyrs were also evidently meant to serve to inspire and encourage their readers. The predominance of young, male protagonists strongly suggests that their intended readership or 'target audience' was likewise young males, who would thus be encouraged to emulate the fidelity, constancy and courage of the saints.

Motif II: **It is the protagonist who initiates his own persecution by openly confessing his Faith, in response to a Divine call to do so.**

In each of the narratives, it is the initiative of the saint which heralds the inception of their persecutions and the events which ultimately lead to their martyrdom. In the cases of St. Epime and St. Apatil, each receives a vision of Christ in which they are called to give public witness of their Faith before the official authorities. For both of these, this is in response to the newly commenced campaign of persecution. Both St. Epime and St. Abanoud make a special journey to an official municipal center for the very purpose of confronting the governor with an open declaration of their faith.

In the case of St. Lacaron, it is stated that he first came to the attention of the authorities by openly declaring himself to be a Christian and not only refusing to worship the pagan deities, but proclaiming to others their falsehood. He is given an opportunity of freeing himself (and even gaining personal advancement) by what the governor himself seems to recognize as a purely 'nominal' acknowledgement of the official gods. The governor says to him:

> *"Offer sacrifice to the gods, and I will let you go free. You are a soldier—and yet you are disloyal to your superiors, by declaring yourself to be a Christian! But we sincerely wish to show you mercy. If you simply make the required sacrifice, you shall be treated with honor."*

In each case, it is evident that the saint deliberately and consciously lets himself enter a perilous situation, by some form of positive action or declaration on his part. Such a bold and confrontational action (which is not without a certain element of humor, perhaps) is when young St. Abanoub hurls a lump of manure into the face of the governor, Lysias, which is recounted thus:

> But immediately, blessed Abanoub picked up off the ground with both hands a huge lump of manure, and hurled it into the face of the governor! As he did so, he exclaimed, "You rabid dog!"

Yet the apparently provocative actions of the saints, in declaring their Faith openly and demonstrating publicly their defiance, were not inspired by any desire for rebellion or disrespect for authority for its own sake. Rather, they take place in response to a clearly articulated Divine vocation. Moreover, they come to serve as an effective public witness to the Gospel, as each of the narratives show. In each case, crowds of people (including members of the public, soldiers, court officials, and, even in one instance, a governor) are converted to Faith in Christ as a result of the visible testimony of courage and endurance which each of the martyrs offers.

Motif III: **There is an incremental progression of the tortures inflicted upon the saints, and their deaths are experiences of peaceful glory.**

On the surface, it may appear that the imperial edict prohibiting Christianity and requiring sacrifice to the official deities could be carried out in a relatively simple manner. Following questioning, if a Christian refused to renounce their Faith they would be promptly put to death. Alternatively, they could be subject to tortures first; and if the tortures did not prevail, they would then be executed. Indeed, the several mentions of mass executions of hundreds and sometimes thousands of Christians indicate that such things were often done in such a straightforward way.

Yet for each of the saints, their progress from their initial confrontation with the authorities to their final end is complex and circuitous, to say the least. They are each subject, not just to one or two tortures, but a veritable proliferation, and these are often horrendous and strange. This is well illustrated by a listing of the multitude of tortures to which St. Apatil is subject before he fulfills his destined martyrdom. His life is the shortest of those contained herein (6,000 words in translation), yet the following incidents befall him:

- He is wrapped in chains and violently pushed around by soldiers, causing him to fall many times; then,

- His ankles are pierced and ropes are threaded through them. He is then dragged over an area of ground covered in sharp gravel; then,

- Still bound, an attempt is made to burn him alive on a bonfire; then,

- He is placed in prison, and sent to a different governor to continue his trials; then,

- His fingernails, toenails and eyeballs are pulled out, and vinegar mixed with ash is poured into his wounds; then,

- He is suspended from a stake and flayed, until his intestines are exposed; then,

- He is bound to an iron bed and a fierce fire is let underneath him; then,

- He is locked in an enclosed furnace, which is set to burn with the greatest possible heat, for some three days; then,

- He is bound in heavy chains, taken out to sea on a boat, and thrown into the deep waters; then,

- He is enclosed in a prison and a beautiful prostitute is sent in, in an attempt to compromise his virtue; then,

- His skin is removed and a hungry lioness is enclosed in the prison cell with him; then,

- He is executed by beheading.

For each of the tortures to which the saints are subject, they are either protected by Christ Himself or by an angel during the torture, or restored to health immediately afterwards. In some cases, these healings are of a drastic and radical nature. For example, after St. Abanoub's body has been cut into three distinct and equal portions by a serrated iron wheel, the archangel Michael appears, and joins the sections of his severed body together once more, and restores him to life and well-being.

In a great many instances, the saint—having either survived or been rescued from a punishment or torture—makes a sudden and surprising re-appearance before the governor, which inevitably results in astonishment, rage and further torments. This occurs literally dozens of times.

Furthermore, the passing of the saint from one authority to another is another constant and conspicuous narrative feature. In the case of St. Abanoud, for example, he is initially tried by the governor Lysias at Gemnuti, then the governor Cyprian at Athribis, and finally by the prince Armenius at Alexandria. Of course, a parallel is apparent here to the handing on of Christ between the Sanhedrin, Herod, and Pontius Pilate. In each case, the transfer of the saint to a higher authority represents and escalation of his torments, and a drawing closer to the consummation of his martyrdom.

In contrast to the complexities of the tortures, the final experience of death itself appears as something remarkably peaceful, inevitable and glorious. In each case, the martyr is taken away to a place of execution and, after being given the opportunity to pray, experiences a vision of Christ, who promises him eternal peace and beatitude. Each saint is beheaded with a single stroke of the sword, with neither pain nor fear. In the case of both St. Epime and St. Abanoub, a mixture of blood and milk flows forth from their body after their decapitation—evidently a symbol of virile strength and courage, combined with the utmost purity and innocence.

Fittingly, death is then followed by an ascent to the Kingdom of Heaven, an event of radiant splendor and ineffable joy. The mystical beauty of this moment of death, which becomes the entrance into eternal glory, is well illustrated at the end of the life of St. Lacaron:

> *The saint then spoke to the executioners, and said to them, "Come and complete the task you have been assigned!" As the executioners approached him, blessed Lacaron stretched out his neck, and they beheaded him. He thus completed his heroic witness to the Faith on the fourteenth day of the month of Paopi.* [6] *And an immense light shone in that place, and a sweet fragrance enveloped it, from the multitude of angels which came to receive the soul of St. Lacaron. And the Savior Himself took his soul up to Heaven with these blessed angels, who followed his ascent. The entire choir of the Heavenly host came to meet them and embraced the martyr, before taking his soul to the celestial city of our Lord, God and Savior, Jesus Christ. To*

6 October 24.

Him be all glory, together with the eternal and gracious Father, and the life-giving Holy Spirit, forever and ever. Amen.

Motif IV: The saint performs numerous healing miracles while in prison, leading to many conversions.

Each of the histories contained in this collection include at least one extended period during which the saint is detained in prison, while the authorities concerned consider how best to proceed with handling his case. In each case, his time of imprisonment proves to be a very fruitful one; the saint performs many healing miracles of a remarkable nature. These lead to numerous conversions, and—what was perhaps very critical in helping finally to undermine the persecution—these conversions included important military and civil officials.

A fine example of this is found in the life of St. Epime. Initially, the saint heals a demoniac, then (through prayer) assists the daughter of a prison guard in delivering her child, and then heals a well-known blind man. Finally, when his reputation has spread through the entire city, a certain high-ranking palace official known as Julius of Aqfahs implores his help to cure his sister Eucharistia, who is afflicted by a demon. This he does, and it leads to the conversion of Julius. This Julius then became the author of the saint's life, and an important hagiographer of other martyrs, before eventually accepting the crown of martyrdom himself. But it is clear both from incidents recounted in the life of St. Epime, as well as that of St. Abanoub, that, even after his conversion, Julius continued to be a respected and influential figure amongst the imperial authorities—presumably on account of his erudition and wisdom, which made them willing to overlook or to tolerate his acceptance of the Christian faith.

In the cases of both St. Epime and St. Apatil, it is related that the healings they performed while being held in prison were so numerous and so remarkable that they inspired a vast outpouring of public support for them throughout the entire city, and a widespread popular embrace of the Christian Faith. It is related of St. Lacaron that, while in prison, he converted all the prisoners there, and presided in ceremonies of common prayer.

This paradoxical transformation of the experience of detention in prison into an enhanced opportunity for Evangelization conveys powerfully the inner or existential freedom which each of the saints possessed in their heart. It shows, indeed, that "God's Word is not held back by chains."[7]

Motif V: Appearances of the Lord Jesus Christ and of angelic beings, especially the archangel Michael.

Appearances of our Lord Jesus Christ and the archangel Michael feature prominently in each of the histories. These appearances always occur as responses to prayers from the saint concerned, and at times of particular crisis or need.

When Christ appears, He is consistently identified with the title 'Savior', reflecting the pertinence of this particular function in moments of desperate and dire need, and especially at the hour of death. And, indeed, He does appear immediately before the death of each of the martyrs whose histories are included in this collection. There is a sense that the authors of the narratives recognize the inadequacy of human words in expressing His ineffable glory and splendor. And in such passages, something of this transcendent and supernal joy is communicated to the reader in a way that surpasses the simplicity of the words employed (or at least thus it seems to the present translator),

---

7   2 Timothy 2:9.

such as in the following, wonderfully radiant passage from the life of St. Abanoub:

> *And behold! At this point, the Savior Himself descended from Heaven, in a chariot of refulgent glory. He was accompanied by the archangels Michael and Gabriel, at His right and at His left respectively, as well as an innumerable multitude of seraphim and cherubim. (…) The Savior then spoke to Abanoub thus: "Be strong, my brave warrior, Abanoub, and take comfort! For I, Jesus your King, am with you. The time of your victory draws nigh, my beloved Abanoub. I have arisen and come to you, so that I may show to you the wonderful crown of light which shall be yours!"*

A similarly beautiful and luminous illustration of this is found in the life of St. Epime:

> *As soon as this prayer was said—behold!—our Lord Jesus Christ appeared before him, with a radiant cloud of light surrounding Him. And the archangel Michael stood at His right hand, while Gabriel was at His left. And the Savior opened his mouth, and spoke thus, "Greetings, Epime, my chosen one! Be brave and take comfort, for I shall be with you in every place to which you are to be led. I am Jesus, your King, who took flesh from the Blessed Virgin Mary. And I shall make your name celebrated throughout the entire orb of the earth. Great wonders and healings will be*

worked through you, and people shall come from
everywhere to venerate your sacred body." And
when the Savior had finished saying this, He
ascended once more into the Heavens in all His
glory. Having seen the Savior, the heart of St.
Epime was filled with immense happiness. And he
exulted with unspeakable joy, giving glory to God.

The archangel Michael also appears at prominent junctures, imparting healing or fortitude to the saints as they undergo their various torments. Indeed, in the present collection, there are no less than seventeen separate appearances of the archangel Michael. As the prince of the Heavenly host, it is only natural that the support and strength of this supernal entity should be present to those who themselves were soldiers by profession (Apatil and Lacaron), but also to those who became soldiers of Christ through holy martyrdom. In the lives of both St. Epime and St. Abanoub, Michael promises them at an early stage that he shall be present with them throughout all the ordeals they shall undergo.

Like the appearances of Christ, the manifestations of the archangel Michael are robed with a radiant luminance, which is both inspiring and touching. This is well illustrated in the following passage from the life of St. Abanoub:

While St. Abanoub was still praying, behold, the
archangel Michael descended from the sky. The
whole place shone with the radiance and gleaming
splendor of the noontide sun. The youth at once fell
upon his face [in awe and surprise], and became
like one who is dead. But Michael touched him
and raised him up to his feet, saying, "Greetings,

good youth, Abanoub, and greetings from God!
O noble man, be strong and take courage. I am
Michael, the commander of the Heavenly army.
The Lord has sent me to strengthen you in the battle
which you shall undergo. "

In addition to these five narrative *motifs*, there are also some features of literary technique and artistry which merit comment. One of these is the profusion of direct speech. Indeed, conversations and dialogues are typically reproduced in much greater detail than one encounters in Latin hagiographies from the same period. Comparatively long discourses and prayers are given, word for word, in each of the histories. The profusion of direct speech functions well as a way of depicting character and personality.

For example, one frequently finds in the speeches of the governors a weak-willed vacillation between admiration of the saint's personal qualities, a desire to win them over, and an insecure arrogance that is ready to flare up into violence with the slightest provocation. For example, Lysias, the governor of Gemnuti, says to St. Abanoub:

> "*I see that you are a handsome and delicate person,*
> *and only a youth. Therefore, you will scarcely be*
> *able to sustain any torture at all. If I struck you*
> *once, I would not need to strike you a second time!*
> *But if you obey me, I shall make you my own son[-*
> *in-law.] I shall promote you to greatness amongst*
> *my eparchs, and many shall honor you, on account*
> *of what I shall do for you. If you give proper worship*
> *to the great god Apollo, I shall give to you [my own*
> *daughter] as your wife!*"

But a few moments later, after Abanoud has declined his proposal, he subjects the saint to a violent flogging. Indeed, in each of the conversations between an imperial authority and a saint, one is left with the impression that it is the saint who is firmly in command of the situation, despite the inequality of worldly power.

Another literary device which is worthy of note is the employment of humor. There are numerous events of an apparently incongruous or bizarre character, which fulfil Schopenhauer's definition of humor as "the sudden incongruity between concept and percept." For example, at one point, in response to the prayer of St. Lacaron, the governor's sandals resume animate form and are transformed into a living calf. In another instance, St. Abanoub commands a serpent to entwine itself around the neck of a governor, which it obediently does. And Magmentius, the governor of Thmuis (who has been converted to Christianity), removes his sandals and places them upon the heads of governor Lysias and Cyprian as a sign of mockery. And the incident (to which reference has already been made) of St. Abanoub hurling manure into the face of governor Lysias is by no means without its humorous aspect.

It is pertinent to make some observations about the texts and the translational approach employed. The source of all the texts is the authoritative 1908 compilation, *Scriptores Coptici, Series Tertia, Tomus I—Acta Martyrum* (edited by I. Balestri and H. Hyvernat), the third volume of the historic *Corpus Scriptorum Christianorum Orientalium* series.[8] The manuscript sources for the texts given in that publication are: for the lives of St. Epime, *Codex Vaticanus Copticus 66*; for the life of St. Abanoub, *Codex Vaticanus Copticus 66*; for the life of St. Apatil, *Codex Vaticanus*

---

8 *Scriptores Coptici, Series Tertia, Tomus I, Corpus Scriptorum Christianorum Orientalium III,* ed. I. Belestri & H. Hyvernat, (Paris: C. Poussielgue, 1913).

Copticus 62; and for the life of St. Lacaron, *Codex Vaticanus Copticus 68.*

The translational approach employed in this present volume is best described as one of 'dynamic equivalence'. Minor mechanical adjustments to word order and syntax have been made wherever it has seemed necessary, desirable or opportune, in order to render the sense of the original faithfully in idiomatic and clear English. This includes the occasional substitution of proper nouns for pronouns, and other such adjustments. A certain degree of judicious freedom has been taken in the choice between various (more or less) synonymous English terms, and in the insertion of adjectives or adverbs where they seem to contribute to the more complete or felicitous communication of the narrative flow or the sense of the original.

Occasionally, it has seemed desirable to make small textual insertions—typically of a phrase or a single sentence—in order to clarify or elucidate the sense. These are indicated by square brackets '[ ]'. Of course, the reader is at liberty to treat such insertions as somewhat conjectural, according to their own judgement and discretion. The chapter divisions included in the lives (indicated by Roman numerals) are all editorial additions.

The approach to translating place names has been to follow the naming given in the original, but to insert the modern equivalents in footnotes wherever possible. The notable exception to this is 'Rhacoti', which has been rendered consistently as 'Alexandria' in the translation. Dates are given in their Coptic form, but the equivalents from the Gregorian calendar (now in general use) have been included in footnotes. Scriptural quotations and allusions are similarly identified in the footnotes.

It is the sincere and earnest hope of the translator that the present volume may inspire, edify and exhort the reader in his or her own life of Faith. Indeed, the persecution of Christians still continues in our contemporary age in many and diverse forms, both overt and covert. May the noble examples and prayers of St. Epime, St Abanoub, St. Apatil and St. Lacaron continue to encourage, assist and fortify us today—shining as a golden ray of celestial light which both promises and leads to that endless day of supernal bliss and peace in the Kingdom of Heaven, which is the inheritance of all true and faithful Christian hearts. And may all glory and honor be given to Jesus Christ, our Lord, God and Savior, together with His Heavenly Father and the Holy Spirit, forever and ever. Amen.

The humble translator,

Rev. Dr. Robert J. Nixon, osb

THE MARTYRDOM OF
ST. EPIME OF PANCOLEUS

by St. Julius of Aqfahs

The Martyrdom of the Strong Warrior of Christ, St. Epime of Pancoleus, in the province of Pemdje,[9] who consummated his blessed battle [for the Faith] on the eighth day of the month of Epip,[10] in the Peace of God. Amen.

I

It happened that during the reign of the emperor Diocletian,[11] that wicked and sinful tyrant, that the devil caused his heart to stray from the One God of Heaven. This happened initially because of a crime committed by a certain archbishop by the name of Gaius, who—having been bribed—had secretly released from prison Nicodemus, the son of Sapor, the king of Persia. And then, with lying oaths, and to conceal his unlawful actions, Gaius had told the story that this Nicodemus [whose true whereabouts were unknown to all] had, in fact, died.

When the emperor heard of this dishonesty on the part of Gaius, he ordered that burning asphalt and pitch should be poured down the throat of this archbishop until he was dead. And after this, now filled with antipathy and disbelief towards the true God of Christianity and all adherents of the Christian religion, Diocletian gathered a vast treasury of pure gold, and had seventy statues fashioned from it. These statues he declared to be gods. The largest and most splendid he called Apollo—and the others he identified as Jupiter, Serapis, Athena, Artemis, and the various other deities of the pagan pantheon.

And Diocletian gathered all his nobles and leading officials to himself, saying: "Listen to me, my friends, for I wish to speak to you all!" They replied, "Please speak to us, O lord and King!"

---

9 Modern day El-Bahnasa
10 July 15.
11 284-305 AD.

And he said to them, "You know that a true king never says that which is false, so believe what I am about to tell you. Last night," he continued, "as I lay down to sleep, it happened that the great god Apollo came to me, and all the other gods following him. And they spoke to me, saying, 'Behold, we have made you strong! We have given you victory in battle. Now you, in return, should glorify us throughout your empire.' So, my friends, what should I do in order to fulfil this instruction from the gods?"

A certain general, Romanus—in fact, the father of St. Victor,[12] [who was, however, still a pagan himself]—said to the emperor, "Hear me, O King, and I shall advise you. In the days of Pharaoh, king of Egypt, people placed their trust in gods which they had fashioned with their own hands, and they still do![13] Let us arise and write an edict to all the people of Egypt, and send it to each of the cities and towns, from Rumania, the city at the northernmost limit of the land, to the most distant city of southern Egypt, Philae, which is next to the country of the Ethiopians. And write to Armenius, the prince of the great metropolis of Alexandria,[14] and the governors of all other cities and towns.

"You should order that all churches consecrated to the name of Christ be destroyed, and that temples for the worship of the Roman gods should be constructed instead in every city and

---

12 Reference is also made to this St. Victor, son of Romanus, as a great wonder-worker in the *Martyrdom of St. Abanoub*.

13 The significance of this comment seems to be that the general Romanus considered the worship of Jesus Christ to be the equivalent of the worship of idols made by human hands, as practiced by the Egyptians in the remote past. The author of the narrative no doubt intends here to highlight ironically the ignorance and misunderstanding of this Romanus.

14 The name given in the Coptic version is Rhacoti. However, since the name Alexandria is so generally known and was already in use at the times of the events recounted in the narrative, it has been employed here, and in all subsequent instances.

village. And command that your troops should assemble all Christian priests, deacons and lectors—together with all the leading city officials—and instruct them that it is absolutely forbidden to offer worship, praise or sacrifice to the Name of Christ. And let them burn with fire every book of Sacred Scripture or of Christian doctrine which they can find!

"Moreover, let pagan priests be appointed, and supplied with funds out of the public treasuries, so that they may open temples, and adore and offer sacrifice to the ancient deities. And if there is anyone who disobeys these commands and refuses to worship the gods, let them be put to the sword or subjected to fire and torture. And let all those who serve as priests of the Christian religion be arrested and brought into the presence of the governor at Alexandria. There, force them to offer worship to the gods—or to die! And let whatever cities, towns and villages do obey these measures be exempted from public taxes and not be required to remit the usual imperial tribute from their agricultural produce."

Now this proposal was most pleasing to emperor Diocletian, who exclaimed, "Through the great god Apollo, let it be done as you have suggested!" He then pronounced a promulgation to this effect against all Christians. Rising early the next morning, which was the first day of the month of Parmouti,[15] he wrote the following decree: "I, Diocletian the Emperor, write to all my kingdom; and the following orders are issued to all who are subject to my command, whether officers, soldiers or civilians. Let the Name of Jesus not be found in the mouth of anyone, and let all worship and make sacrifice to the great gods of Rome." And thus it was done.

Now there was in those times a young soldier, the son of a certain high-ranking officer, who read the decree of Diocletian. And when he did, he cried out and wept fervently, saying, "O

---

15 April 9.

my Lord Jesus Christ, help me! Light within me a lamp of truth, that I may be able to speak to this atheistic Emperor who seeks to vituperate your most holy Name, and make him see his error."

Having said this, he removed his official belt, and hastened to the imperial palace. There, he went in boldly and gained entrance to the presence of the emperor himself, who said to him, "Who are you, that you thus [boldly] stand before me?"

The youth replied, "My name is Christodorus, and I have been your soldier, and am the son of your officer, Basilides." Diocletian, surprised, said to him in anger, "And how is it that you dare to stand before me not wearing your official belt of military service?! Do you wish to disgrace the honor of your distinguished father?"

Christodorus answered him, "O wicked king! From this moment onwards I am no longer your soldier, because I know that the devil has planted his root within you. I proudly affirm my Faith in the Lord Jesus Christ, who made Heaven and earth, and the sea and the rivers, and all the creatures contained therein! And He created me too, and my life is in His hands."

When Diocletian heard the youth saying these things, he was overcome by violent rage. Rising to his feet, he seized a sword from a soldier who was standing nearby, and thrust it through the chest of the young Christian, killing him at once. Then he ordered his troops to come to him, and to cut the body of the young man to pieces, limb by limb.

And thus Christodorus achieved holy martyrdom on that day— his soul flying from the edge of the bloody sword of the tyrant, to the glorious light of Heaven. And there, indeed, he now rests in eternal peace amongst all the saints of God! Amen.

After this, the Emperor commanded that all altars consecrated to Christ be burnt, and that all his armies should offer incense to the pagan deities. And on a single day, six thousand soldiers and thirty thousand civilians worshiped these impure idols. Indeed, all those in the city of Rome—men and women, children and adults—240,000 altogether, offered adoration to Diocletian's false divinities.

And he wrote an edict, giving it to one of his generals, named Dionysius. He ordered him to take it to Alexandria, to the prince of that city, Armenius. The edict read thus:

> *I, Emperor Diocletian, write to Armenius, the prince of Alexandria. Because the immortal gods have bestowed upon me such triumphs and dignity, I order you to destroy all Christian churches forthwith. And I command that you raise up worthy temples, in which the immortal gods shall be adored by all the citizens, and offerings of incense be made unto them. This is to take place not only in the great city of Alexandria, but also to be extended as far as Aswan in the south, and to the west as far as the Pentapolis of Libya. If any should be so rebellious as to disobey this decree, and refuse to pay homage to the gods of Rome, I command that you should subject them to the most severe tortures. After this, they are to be put to death by the sword.*

When the general Dionysius had entered Alexandria, he handed the decree to Armenius. And Armenius, in turn, ordered all the citizens of Alexandria to gather together, and he read to them the imperial edict. He then wrote letters to the leaders of all the provinces, cities and towns of the entire land of Egypt. Accordingly, a letter from Armenius was presented to Culcianus, the governor of the province of Pemdje. Culcianus studied it carefully, and found it to read thus: "I grant to you the power to kill whomsoever shall refuse to obey the orders of the Emperor. Alternatively, you may send them to me here at Alexandria, and I shall have them tortured."

Whenever God wills to test and prove the Faith of His chosen ones—that is to say, the Christian people—He does so according to the dispositions of His almighty will, in order that He may make known the radiant glory of His Church. God often does this by letting His saints suffer for the sake of His most blessed Name. Indeed, by this means they are granted sure entrance into the splendid bliss of Heaven. It was on account of such martyrs that the Apostle Paul said, "A cloud of witnesses is granted to us,"[16] and similarly that the prophet Isaiah wrote, "Let those who wish to be taught by God come unto me".[17] And it was for this very reason that God had permitted an evil spirit to enter the heart of Diocletian, so that His own servants might attain to the glory of martyrdom.

In the past, He had done the same with Pharaoh, when He hardened his heart against the people of Israel. And in those days, it was the Israelites whom God liberated, whilst Pharaoh and his troops He destroyed in the waters of the Red Sea. And so it was with this evil king Diocletian, who so sorely provoked the wrath of God and His holy angels. But because of this, the faithful saints of God were able to become heirs to the Kingdom of Heaven, and receive the reward of eternal life.

---

16 Cf. Hebrews 12:1.
17 Cf. Isaiah 54:13.

II

Hear, therefore, all you who have ears to hear! Hear, all you who have intelligence! For you know that nothing is sweeter than the holy Name of Jesus, and nothing is more glorious than the honor of being a true Christian.

There was a certain farmer by the name of Epime, in a village called Pancoleus, in the province of Pemdje.[18] His parents were both good Christians. The name of his father was Elias, and the name of his mother was Sophia. He himself was a righteous and faithful man, avoiding all evil, wise, a lover of charity, and giving the first fruits of all his produce and profits to the House of God. And the Word of God was to him as honey in his mouth, and a brilliant light burning deep inside him. Indeed, his way of life was as if he was already living in Heaven. And he was filled with every virtue of the Holy Spirit.

Now, all the common people loved and revered him for his good works, and he was respected as a leader of his community. Though he was a humble man, his reputation and fame as an exemplary Christian was widespread. But for this very reason, the officials, officers and magistrates who had been charged with

---

18 Modern day El-Bahnasa.

carrying out Diocletian's cruel campaign of persecution came to seek him out zealously.

One night when Epime was sleeping quietly in his house, he saw a vision of a splendid youth standing over him, who gently touched him on the right side and woke him up. Epime instantly was roused from his slumber, and, seeing the unexpected figure of this radiant young man standing before him, was struck with fear and astonishment. But the man said to him, "Epime, open your eyes, and you shall see who I am!

> *"I am Christ, whose glowing dawn rises in the east!*
>
> *I am Christ, whose radiant star the Magi beheld and adored!*
>
> *I am Christ, whom the blessed Virgin Mary bore!*
>
> *I am Christ, the glorious crown of the martyrs!*
>
> *"For the sake of my Name, you shall undergo much suffering; but I shall make your own name to be celebrated and revered throughout the whole world. Arise, and go to the governor! Openly confess your Faith to him; and fear not, for I myself am with you. The Divine peace which my Father gave to me when I went out from Him, I also give to you!"*

And when the Savior had said all these things, He made a sign of blessing over Epime, so that no pain of torture should be able to touch his body. He then ascended upwards into the Heavens, whilst Epime looked on.

At the first light of dawn the next morning, St. Epime arose, and went forth from his parents' house. However, he told no one in his family about the vision he had seen during the previous night, lest they should try to prevent him from doing that which he intended. Rather, he told them, "I am going to the markets at Pemdje today, for I need to purchase an ox." And they replied, "Go in peace, Epime. And may God send His angel before you, that your journey may be well directed."

Epime then set out. Turning his face to the east, he prayed to God, saying, "My Lord, Jesus Christ, Son of the living God! Hear me today calling to you in Heaven. For you once said, 'Whoever does not give up father and mother, his brother and sisters, his wife and children and fields, and take up his cross and follow Me, is not worthy of Me.'[19] Lord, You know that I have given up everything I possess for You, so that I may follow You completely.

"O Lord, do not close to me the doors of Your justice! Grant strength to me, that I may be able to fulfil whatever You command—for to You belong all glory and power, with the Father and the Holy Spirit, forever and ever. Amen."

And when he had completed his prayer, he blessed himself with the sign of the cross, in the name of the Father, the Son and the Holy Spirit, and continued on his way.

Once St. Epime had entered the city of Pemdje, he heard that the local governor, Culcianus, was holding his tribunal of judgement at the tetrapylon,[20] and hearing the trials of several Christians. The names of these were Pihop, a deacon from the village of Canas; Hor, a monk from the village of Togensis; Maximus, a priest from Senero; and Penthos, a deacon from Terbensis. There were also many members of the laity, from the entire province. When Epime saw all that was taking place, he raised his eyes to Heaven, and prayed, "O my Lord Christ, give

---

19 Cf. Matthew 10:38.

20 A place of public assembly, consisting of four large pillars with a roof on top.

me strength and fortitude, so that I may be able to speak to this wicked governor!"

Now, while Epime was praying thus, a certain municipal guard, Abianus, saw him standing there. Abianus at once stepped out before the governor and said, "Your Excellency, look! Here is Epime, the head of the Christians in Pancoleus, standing right before you. I propose that he be ordered to bring to us all the clerics and deacons of his village, as well as all the sacred vessels of his Church, together with their Scriptures, altars and chalices, and whatever else the Emperor has commanded."

Culcianus quite agreed with this suggestion and immediately he sent his attaché, a man called Theodore, to arrest Epime and bring him before his tribunal. And the governor questioned him thus, "Are you Epime, the head of the community at Pancoleus?" Epime replied, "Yes, certainly I am."

The governor continued, "And which of the gods do you worship? Is it Apollo, perhaps, or Jupiter? Choose one, and let your choice save you!" But Epime replied, "I place my Faith in none of these, but only in the God of Heaven, my Father and Lord, Jesus Christ!"

Upon hearing this, the governor frowned darkly. "Well," he said, "in that case, I must order you to bring to me all your priests and deacons and vessels of the altar." Epime answered him honestly, "We have no priests in our village. Rather, I travel around the surrounding areas to find someone who is able to give to us Communion on each Sabbath and Sunday. And the sacred vessels which we use for Communion are not of precious metal, but merely of glass. Indeed, we are all extremely poor, and barely able to support ourselves by our small farmlands."

The governor, suspecting Epime of lying to him, then became enraged. He snapped, "Epime, you are not able to mock me with these deceptions! For already there are those who have warned me about the falsehood which is lurking within you. Do precisely as I have instructed you—bring me your priests and deacons and sacred vessels! Otherwise, I warn you, your flesh shall feel the most bitter of tortures."

St. Epime answered him with perfect calmness and courage. "My Lord Jesus Christ has already shown me that these things would happen to me, and He said to me, 'Do not fear those who can kill your body, but do not have the power to destroy your soul'.[21]" When he heard this the governor asked him, "Do you really want to lose your flesh?" But the saint replied, "Do to me whatever you wish. For my Lord Jesus Christ is with me, and He shall give me strength to endure anything!"

Calcianus then threatened him, "I shall cut out your tongue, Epime, before you can once more utter the name of Jesus in my presence!" To this, the saint replied, "Certainly, do so! For you are, indeed, not worthy to hear the most holy Name of my Lord Jesus Christ." At this point, the governor was overcome with violent wrath, and ordered a sharpened razor to be brought to them, and Epime's tongue to be cut out forthwith, his feet to be bound in chains, and him to be cast into a dungeon until morning.

Having been imprisoned in the dungeon in the governor's palace, Epime raised his hands to God. Although, since his tongue had been cut out, he could not pray with words, yet still he prayed in his heart, and glorified the Lord. And—behold!—the Archangel Michael appeared before him, and made a sign upon his mouth. And instantly Epime's tongue was restored, and he could speak perfectly. And immediately he broke forth in loud praise of God, so that all who were in prison with him heard him quite clearly.

---

21 Matthew 10:28.

III

The next morning, governor Culcianus sat in his hall of judgement and ordered St. Epime to be brought before him, so that he might formally determine his case. But when he entered and was heard to be able to speak, the governor was astounded. Taken aback, he said to him, "Come now, Epime! Make the proper sacrifice to the official gods, and I shall let you go free." But Epime was not to be persuaded, and retorted, "Far be it from me ever to worship your impure idols! But I shall worship and adore only my Lord Jesus Christ, and none other."

Then the fires of rage again flared up in the heart of the governor. He ordered Epime to be suspended alive from the gallows, and to be afflicted with all forms of tortures. As the guards prepared to suspend him, Epime faithfully signed himself with the cross, in the name of the Father, the Son and the Holy Spirit. And then he was suspended by ropes, while he was subject to whips, scourges and all instruments of cruelty and torment. This was continued ruthlessly and mercilessly, to the point that his entrails and bones were exposed to view, and all his body totally soaked in blood. But, still hanging there, he raised his eyes to Heaven, and prayed, "My Lord Jesus Christ, help me in this, my hour of pain!"

As soon as he had offered this prayer, his heart was strengthened and he cried out more loudly, "Be ashamed, you wretched Culcianus, for you are equally wicked as the godless emperor whom you serve!" And he seemed to care nothing about all the tortures which were being inflicted upon his body.

Seeing this cruel and inhuman spectacle and the courage of the saint, all the citizens cried out, execrating Diocletian and his impure idols. At this point, Culcianus ordered that Epime be taken down, and returned to his prison cell. And so it was done.

That night, as Epime lay in the blackness of his dungeon cell, suddenly the archangel Michael appeared to him, surrounded by brilliant light. And he said, "Peace be with you! It is the Lord who has sent me to you, so that I may heal you." Then the archangel extended his hand over the wounded body of the saint and made a sign over him. And instantly he was restored to perfect soundness and strength, with Michael saying, "Do not fear, for I shall remain with you until you have completed your battle!" And the heart of St. Epime was filled with joy. He spent the whole night in prayer and blessing the Lord, until the light of dawn arose.

But once morning had arrived, Culcianus again sat at his tribunal of judgement, and called for Epime to be brought before him again. When the guards had led him in, the governor saw him, looking perfectly joyful and healthy, as if he had just come in from enjoying a banquet! He was filled with wonder at this amazing thing, and exclaimed to him, "You are still alive?! Indeed, you are assuredly a very great magician." However, [despite being impressed by Epime's miraculous survival of the torture and complete physical healing,] he persisted in his demands that he render sacrifice to the pagan divinities. "Sacrifice to the gods, or I shall be compelled to torture you again."

But Epime responded, "Do to me whatever you wish, for I have my Lord Jesus Christ who shall strengthen and protect me against anything which you do to me. It is written, 'All who worship gods made by human hands and glory in their idols shall be confounded'.[22]"

Now Culcianus was again seized by fury and indignation. He commanded that Epime should be made to sit on a chair of iron, and a metal helmet—made red hot by fire—should be placed on his head. Meanwhile, burning lamps were to be applied to his sides. After this, continued the governor, two long nails—also heated in fire—were to be forced through his shoulders, until they reached the back of the chair on which he sat.

As the guards began to carry out this gruesome torture, Epime blessed himself with the invincible sign of the Father, the Son and the Holy Spirit. And at once, the heated helmet was transformed into a harmless but precious crown of beautiful pearls, and the burning lamps reversed themselves—burning, not Epime, but the guards who held them.

Now a crowd of citizens, upon perceiving these wonders, at once broke out with cries, shouting at the governor, "The God of the Christians is truly great, for He can bestow such strength upon His holy ones! We shall not permit you to slaughter this just man in our city!"

When the governor heard this, he was struck by fear of the determined crowd of citizens. He saw also the guards who had been holding the lamps, now both set ablaze themselves. And so he turned to the saint and spoke to him in desperation and panic. "I adjure you", said he, "in the name of your Jesus, through whom you can do such marvelous deeds, order that these lamps stop burning my guards, for they are now being tortured by the flames that were meant for you."

---

22 Psalm 97:7.

At once, Epime raised his eyes to Heaven and prayed, "Give ear to me, my Lord Jesus Christ! You yourself were tortured by the Jews, at the time when you were hung from the cross. And you prayed to Your own Divine Father, saying, 'Forgive them, for they know not what they do.'[23] Now, therefore, Lord, this is the hour in which Your own great Name will again be glorified!"

After he had said this, he approached the guards and made the sign of the cross over them, saying, "May the Lord Jesus Christ make this fire withdraw from you!" And at once the fire vanished, and the guards were saved.

The governor Culcianus, amazed at the miraculous deeds performed at the hands of Epime, asked him with great curiosity about the sign of the cross. "Will you please show me that sign which you just made, and which you make so frequently upon yourself? Indeed, you are a very great wonder-worker, and I have never seen anyone perform such deeds as you, or make that sign which you use. In the name of your God, Jesus, I adjure you to speak to me the truth!"

Epime answered him thus, "Pay attention to me, for I shall show you the sign." And he demonstrated to Culcianus how to make the sign of the cross. He continued, "This was the sign which God made over the first human being when He created him, and this is also the sign which my Lord Jesus Christ gave to all His followers who believe—in Him, the Son; and in the Father and in the Holy Spirit."

The governor then turned to an advisor, and asked him, "What shall we do with this man, now that all the crowd is crying out in his favor? Indeed, they have declared firmly that they will not permit us to torture or execute him within the boundaries of this city." The advisor considered carefully, and replied, "Your

---

23 Luke 23:34.

Excellency, I advise you thus: send him to Alexandria—to Armenius, the prince of that great metropolis. And his tortures and punishment can be continued there, if the prince sees fit to do so."

This suggestion greatly pleased Culcianus, who wrote to Armenius in the following terms:

> *I, Culcianus, the governor of Pemdje, write to my beloved brother Armenius, the noble prince of Alexandria. Greetings to you! I wish to communicate to you about this man Epime, who is guilty of professing and practicing the Christian faith. He is from the village of Pancoleus, within my own province of Pemdje, and is a leader of his community. Indeed, all obey him, because of the great magical arts which he has mastered. And, because of the wondrous works he has performed, the citizens of Pemdje will not permit me to torture or execute him here. Therefore, I send him to you, that you may deal with him as Your Excellency sees fit; and administer due punishment, should he refuse to obey the decrees of our Emperor.*

Once Culcianus had completed writing this letter, he ordered that Epime's hands be tied behind his back, a chain be placed around his neck, and his nose be pierced and a ring placed in it [as is the custom for marking prisoners]. And then he ordered him to be sent without delay to Armenius, the prince of Alexandria.

When Epime had been transferred to a ship destined for that city, the sailors placed his feet in iron fetters, and cast him into the hull of the ship, and set sail on their northward voyage. Now the saint, as he lay bound in the dark hull of the ship, felt utterly dejected in his heart. But raising his eyes to Heaven, he prayed, "O my Lord Jesus Christ, be with me as a helper throughout all the difficult paths upon which I shall be led."

As soon as this prayer was said—behold!—our Lord Jesus Christ appeared before him, with a radiant cloud of light surrounding Him. And the archangel Michael stood at His right hand, while Gabriel was at His left. And the Savior opened his mouth, and spoke thus, "Greetings, Epime, my chosen one! Be brave and take comfort, for I shall be with you in every place to which you are to be led. I am Jesus, your King, who took flesh from the Blessed Virgin Mary. And I shall make your name celebrated throughout the entire orb of the earth. Great wonders and healings will be worked through you, and people shall come from everywhere to venerate your sacred body." And when the Savior had finished saying this, He ascended once more into the Heavens in all His glory.

Having seen the Savior, the heart of St. Epime was filled with immense happiness. And he exulted with unspeakable joy, giving glory to God.

IV

Very quickly, the ship completed its voyage and arrived at Alexandria. The soldiers who had been entrusted with keeping custody of Epime left the ship with their prisoner, and went to seek Armenius, the prince and ruler of the city. And they found him seated at the civic stadium, watching the spectacle of the cruel public slaughter of criminals and captives. Indeed, that day happened to be the birthday of the emperor, and such bloody spectacles were part of the customary celebrations. The soldiers handed to Armenius the letter written to him by Culcianus concerning Epime, who himself followed them, with his hands tied behind his back, a chain around his neck and a ring through his nose.

Armenius read the letter, and was eager to hear Epime's case on that very day. But the citizens protested, not wishing the spectacle then taking place at the stadium to be interrupted. So Armenius ordered him to be placed in prison, so that his case could be heard the next day.

Accordingly, Epime was placed in the prison of Alexandria that night. Now there was also being held in that prison cell a certain man, by the name of Dionysius, son of Theodore, who was possessed by a malignant demon. When he saw Epime, he cried out "No longer shall I return to enter into you, O Dionysius, son of Theodore! For I see here to be present the mighty archangel Michael himself standing next to you, Epime. Out of fear of him, I no longer dare to remain in this place!" And immediately the demon threw the man to the ground and went forth from him. At this, the heart of Dionysius recovered its strength, and he fell at the feet of the saint, giving thanks and homage to him. And the prison guard saw all this take place, and was filled with great wonder.

This same prison guard had only one child, a daughter. Now this daughter of his was pregnant, and had come to the time at which she was due to give birth. But she had been in labor for three days already without delivering her child, and was quickly reaching the point of death. When her father saw the miracle which had taken place at the hands of the saint, he fell to his feet and implored him to come to the assistance of his daughter. St. Epime said to him, "Bring to me a little oil and I shall pray over it, so that the glory of my Lord Jesus Christ may be manifested through it." The guard quickly brought the requested oil, and the saint prayed over it, saying, "O Jesus Christ, my Lord and God! Have mercy upon the work of Your hands, for all power belongs to You—and, through this thing, may Your Name be glorified, with the Father and the Holy Spirit, forever and ever. Amen."

Once he had completed this prayer and made the sign of the cross over the oil, he directed that it be taken to the girl and she be anointed with it. This was done, and immediately she bore a son without further difficulty. And she named him Epime, after the holy man through whose intercession the child had been born and her own life saved.

Now there was a certain blind man, who sat at the gates of the prison begging alms from all who passed by. When he heard of the wonders which had been worked through St. Epime, he arose and went to him, beseeching him earnestly that he should restore to him his sight. Epime turned to the man, and prayed over him, saying, "O God, who opened the eyes of the man born blind at Bethpage, and who restored sight to two blind beggars who besought your aid, hear me also! Lord, have mercy and grant to this man his sight, for he has truly placed his hopes in you." And, as soon as Epime made the sign of the cross, in the name of the Father, the Son and the Holy Spirit, over the blind man, his eyes were opened and he saw perfectly. And this man went throughout the whole of the city, vociferously proclaiming the marvelous things which had been done for him through this holy man. And so the saint's fame spread amongst all the people.

There was at that time a certain high-ranking government official by the name of Julius, who had a virgin sister, named Eucharistia. The devil came to envy this woman, because of all the good works she did, and came to take possession of her. As a result of this demonic possession, her whole body was tormented and contorted. Her right hand was twisted down to her right foot, and her frame became withered and distorted. For some fourteen years she had been confined to her bed, for she could no longer raise herself to her feet.

When Julius heard of the wondrous healings which the saint had performed from prison, he made haste to visit him. He sought his assistance earnestly, saying, "O holy man, I have heard of the miracles which you have done in the Name of Christ. I have a sister whom the devil, inflamed by envy at her good works, has afflicted with grave infirmity throughout her whole body. For the last fourteen years, she has been confined to her bed, unable to support herself on her feet. I have had a veritable multitude of doctors and magicians see her, but not one has been able to heal her. But if you pray to your God for her and she is restored to health, whatever you ask of me, I shall do for you. If you wish for me to organize your release so that you may return to your own home in peace, I shall see the prince Armenius and pay him three pounds of pure gold, and he shall certainly release you. Please, do this simple favor for me!"

Upon hearing this, St. Epime laughed, and said, "I certainly do not wish to be set free, for it was not human power that led me here, but rather the will of God Himself! But there is another good work which I would ask of you—when the sentence of death has been carried out upon me, take care of my body, and see to it that it is sent back to my own village, to be laid amongst the tombs of my ancestors and my kinsfolk." Julius replied, "Certainly, I shall do that for you. And I ask that you will kindly remember me in the glorious Heaven to which you shall surely go!"

And Epime opened his mouth and blessed Julius, saying, "May the God and Father of my Lord Jesus Christ bless you, Julius, my dear brother. May hunger and disease never enter your household, and may your descendants be forever free from all affliction." Once he had concluded this blessing, he continued speaking to Julius, "Send your sister to me here, that the glory of God may be made manifest through her."

Julius then sent some of his servants, who collected his sister and brought her into the presence of the saint in the prison. Epime then took a vessel of water and prayed over it, saying, "I beseech you, my Lord Jesus Christ, from whom alone all health and life comes! Hear me praying to you today, and mercifully bestow health and well-being upon this good woman, Eucharistia, the sister of Julius, for all the good works which she has done for your holy ones in the past." And immediately he made the sign of the cross over her with water, and had the servants pour the remainder of the water over her body. And immediately, she was able to rise up, and stood firmly on her feet. She gave glory to God, and poured out thanks and praise to St. Epime.

Indeed, while St. Epime was being held in prison in Alexandria, he performed—in addition to these described here—a great many other miraculous healings.

Armenius, the prince of Alexandria, soon came to hear about these various prodigies which Epime had performed from his prison. And so he commanded his tribunal of judgement to be set up in the place which is called Cisarion, and Epime to be brought there to appear before him. And when this was done, he addressed him thus, "Are you Epime, the renowned magician?"

The saint replied, "Certainly, I am Epime. But I am no magician. Rather, I am a servant of my Lord Jesus Christ, the Son of the living God!" Armenius then asked him, "What are these works then, which you have performed while in prison?"

The saint responded, "The works which I have done are not the result of any magical arts, but are done purely through the mighty Name of Christ."

"Let me tell you," continued Epime, "the story of one who practiced magic. I have heard that there was a certain magician, Astrolole by name, who did amazing deeds by means of his art. Now, once when he had made an invocation, a great well, opening to unfathomable depths, suddenly opened before him. Wishing to explore the things that lay hidden therein, he descended into it. But when he had entered the well, a host of demons seized him. Some shouted, 'Let us kill him!', while others exclaimed, 'Let us tear his skin off him!' In one word, they sought to inflict all kinds of torment and harm upon him. Astrolole, meanwhile, called upon all the magical powers and occult entities he could think of, but not a single one prevailed to assist him. Finally, he remembered the God of the Christians, and his heart took courage. He said to himself, 'If the very thought of the God of the Christians is able to give courage to my heart, how much more may He be able to help me if I call upon His name?'

"So the magician immediately cried out, 'O Jesus Christ, God of the Christians! If you free me from this morass of peril in which I currently find myself, I shall willingly pour out my very blood for your holy Name!' And the mouth of the well was opened, and he was drawn up safely out of the abyss.

"O foolish and ignorant man! You may learn from the story I have just told you that there is no deity with the power to save, except for the God of the Christians. He alone is able to destroy all the enchantments and spells of the devil, by which the arch-fiend strives to deceive humankind."

Having listened attentively to this story, Armenius said to Epime, "Please listen to me. If you simply offer the customary sacrifices to the official gods, I shall be happy to let you go free at once." But the saint replied, "May you be satisfied with my words. Let it be known to you that I shall never offer sacrifice to your impure idols!"

At this point, Armenius became irritated by his determination, and raised his voice to Epime. "Hear my advice! Make sacrifices to the gods, or I shall have no choice but to hand you over to be tortured. But if you agree, and ask anything of me, I promise I shall do it for you. For, indeed, I am personally concerned about your case."

The saint enquired of him, "And what kind of favor do you imagine I might ask of you?" The governor replied, "Well, if you wished, you could ask me to write to the emperor about your merits, and he would confer suitable honors and dignities upon you—perhaps assigning a hundred soldiers to you, to do your bidding." The saint laughed, and answered him, "Do you really think I am interested in anything like that? Verily, my God lives forever! Even if the emperor were to give me a hundred soldiers and these hundred soldiers should serve me for one hundred years, all of these one hundred years would not be worth a single hour in the Kingdom which my Lord Jesus Christ has prepared for those who love Him!"

Upon hearing this, Armenius became inflamed by fierce wrath, and commanded that Epime should be suspended alive from the gallows, and tortured until his bones were exposed. But the saint, having been suspended from the gallows, raised his eyes to Heaven and cried out, saying, "My Lord Jesus Christ, help me in this calamity into which I have fallen!"

And while he still prayed—behold!—the Archangel Michael suddenly appeared in the form of a dove of the most radiant whiteness, which settled upon the head of the saint. And immediately the chains and ropes which held him crumbled into dust, and the gallows itself broke into two parts. And there stood Epime before the tribunal, freed from his bonds and completely unharmed!

Armenius, his commands having apparently been thwarted, was furious. He ordered Epime to be tortured yet again. This time, he instructed that a great pit of fire be constructed and the saint to be lowered into it by means of iron shackles, until his skin was completely incinerated. This was done—but Epime remained entirely unharmed, even in the midst of the ferocious flames.

He then commanded that the saint's fingernails and toenails be torn out, one by one, and vinegar and ashes to be poured upon the wounds. Furthermore, he ordered his male member to be cut off and fried in boiling oil. These tortures were all carried out, but Epime bore them with courage and fortitude. After this, Armenius instructed for lead to be melted over a furnace, and the molten metal to be poured down Epime's throat.

The noble saint spoke to the cruel governor, "O foolish and wicked man! I am like one who has just been out in the hot winds, and who then imbibes cool water with delight! For thus does this molten lead seem to me now, and I drink it easily."

The governor was insane with rage, and ordered nails to be driven through Epime's hands and feet, and him to be dragged through the city square, until the dust of the earth was soaked with his blood. The soldiers took him away to do this gruesome thing, but shortly they returned. And there stood Epime with them, completely unharmed! And the crowd of citizens, who had witnessed all these things, acclaimed in amazement, "There is no god, but the God of the Christians!"

V

Armenius was infuriated at hearing the crowd proclaim God in this way, and declared proudly, "By the great Apollo! Even if Epime's God has got two right hands, He shall not be able to save him from my power! Nevertheless, for the sake of the emperor's justice, I shall not finish him off yet, until I have seen a full demonstration of the power of his God."

Upon hearing this, the saint said to the governor, "Because you have blasphemed against my God, He shall inflict a penalty upon you. You shall become mute, and not be able to utter any further words of sacrilege." And immediately the lips of Armenius became tightly fused and his tongue paralyzed, so that he was unable to make a single sound. And the crowd cried out all the more fervently, "Truly, there is no god except for the Lord Jesus Christ, the God of the Christians!"

Then Armenius arose, and sought out his wise official, Julius—the same man whose sister Epime had liberated from demonic possession earlier. Communicating by means of writing, he begged him that he persuade St. Epime to heal him from the infirmity by which he was now afflicted. Julius then approached Epime, and embraced him with fraternal affection, kissing him on the chest. He begged him earnestly, "I beseech you, O martyr of Christ, heal our leader Armenius." The saint replied, "The Lord Christ, whom he has blasphemed, is a God who lives! Armenius shall not be able to speak anymore, until he takes a pen, ink and paper, and writes with his own hand, professing there to be no deity, except for the Lord Jesus Christ, the God of the Christians."

So Armenius accordingly took a sheet of paper, pen and ink, and sat down and wrote thus: "I hereby declare that I believe there to be no deity, except for the Lord Jesus Christ, the God of the Christians." And all who were present took the sheet of paper and carefully examined the text that the prince had written. Then St. Epime was brought into his presence, and having read the declaration himself, said, "In the name of my Lord Jesus Christ, O God of the Christians, who once opened the mouth of your priest Zachariah so that he could speak and glorify your name;[24], O Lord, open the mouth of this man, that he may speak once again, and say whatsoever he wishes. Indeed, I know that he does not genuinely believe in you. But I ask this on account of the multitude that is here assembled, that they may witness this work and come to believe in Your holy Name!"

And immediately the mouth of Armenius was opened and his faculty of speech returned. Nevertheless his heart was darkened with pride and anger, and he said, "You audacious scoundrel! You have exerted all your powers against me this day. But I shall not spare your life!"

The governor then commanded that Epime be led off to the city bathhouse. There his hands and feet were to be bound, and the saint to be cast into the furnace and a fire to be lighted around him. And thus it was done. Epime was bound and thrown into the furnace, amidst blazing flames. And he remained there for some three days and three nights.

---

24 Cf. Luke 1:64.

Surrounded by the fierce fires, Epime prayed to God, saying, "O God, you listened to the prayers of the patriarch Abraham, and extinguished the fire of King Bosoch which burnt around him. And you rescued your saints Paul and Thecla from the flames of Thamyris. You saved Joseph from the hands of Pharaoh, and you sent your angel to rescue the three young men from the blazing furnace of the evil King Nebuchadnezzar. And that king was ready to confess your name, saying, 'Did we not cast three young men, bound, into the fire? And yet I behold four of them walking around in the middle of the flames, quite unharmed. And the fourth one looks like the Son of God!'[25] Now, my Lord, listen to my plea, and free me from the midst of this fire—for this day is to me truly a day of wrath, a day of tribulation, and a day of anxiety!"

And—behold! —the archangel Michael appeared that very instant, descending from Heaven above and entering into the blazing furnace. This celestial being drew near to Epime and spread over him his radiant wings. At once, the flames became like a cool dewfall, carried by the first gentle breeze at the hour of dawn. And the Archangel spoke to the holy man, "Be strong and take courage, O athlete of Christ! For I am Michael, whom the Lord has sent to you, that I should assist and protect you from all harm." And the chains and ropes fell from Epime, and he arose and stood on his feet, quite unharmed.

Meanwhile—when Epime had been in the furnace for three days, all the while protected by the angel of the Lord—Armenius happened to make a visit to the bathhouse, wishing to wash himself there. As he removed his garments and bathed, he suddenly recalled Epime. Assuming him to be dead, he laughed to himself, saying, "Ah, Epime, you must be regretting your

---

25 Daniel 3:24-25.

foolishness now! For where was your God to free you from your fate at my hands?"

But just as he was saying this to himself, the archangel Michael took Epime from the furnace and stood him before Armenius, not only alive but completely unharmed. The governor, enraged and embarrassed, at once got up and left the bathhouse without completing his ablutions. But the saint boldly followed, [mockingly] walking behind him throughout the squares of the city. And all the townspeople saw him, and were filled with amazement.

In those days, there was a man called Eusebius, a leading citizen of Alexandria, who was having a villa built for himself in the city. His only son had been put in charge of supervising the construction, and was urging the builders on with their work. Now, at the time when St. Epime was passing by the site, the youth happen to fall from the top of the building. His head struck the ground with such force that his brain was ruptured within his skull, and began to run out through his nostrils. Indeed, his entire body was as if it had been violently shattered by the impact. A crowd had gathered around the lifeless remains of the unfortunate youth, weeping and lamenting in shock and sorrow.

Now St. Epime observed what had happened, and approached, speaking to the crowd, "Draw back from him, that the glory of the Lord Jesus Christ may be manifested through him!" The crowd withdrew a little, and the saint stood above the body of the unfortunate adolescent, and prayed in a forceful voice, "My Lord Jesus Christ! Hear my prayer, so that your glory may be exhibited to this multitude." And he took the hand of the young man, and raised him up. And—behold!—his body was restored to perfect wholeness. His heart began to beat within him once more, and he opened his eyes, quite alive. And seeing

Epime before him, he blessed him and blessed God. And the whole crowd who were assembled and witnessed the incident gave glory to God and venerated His saint, who was capable of performing such wonders.

After this had transpired, immediately a group of some one-hundred and six men went to the prince and rushed into his palace, crying out loudly, "There is one God only, the God of the Christians, Jesus Christ—who is the God of St. Epime! This is the God in whom we hope, and who has confounded you and your emperor and your idols! We proclaim ourselves openly to be Christians. We are dedicated to the almighty God whom St. Epime serves."

Armenius was enraged, and ordered the whole crowd to be led to the sea, and there to be put to death. He said to his executioner, Symmachus, "Go with this rabble of traitors, and carry out upon them the sentence of death prescribed by the imperial edict. And I grant to you full authority to kill them all, in whatever manner pleases you the most!"

So Symmachus the executioner led this crowd of holy martyrs to the seashore, and had them arrange themselves in lines. He seized his sword, and as he went along, some he beheaded, others he dismembered, while others he thrust through with the blade. In other words, he dispatched each one as the whim took him. After killing a few in this manner, he was fatigued and sat down on a stone to rest for a while.

One of the crowd of Christians, Dioscorus by name, raised his voice, and spoke to the executioner. "Symmachus, my son, cease to pour out the blood of holy ones in this way! For great indeed is their God, and He shall not excuse you for this crime, but will hold you responsible for their blood." But Symmachus replied contemptuously, "Oh well! If I die, let the pupil of my right eye be placed under the doorway of hell!" And all the blessed ones present who still lived said, "Amen! It shall indeed be done to you just as you have said."

Symmachus arose, and continued with his ghastly work of killing, until all the faithful crowd were martyred. And the firmament that day was filled with angels, who descended from Heaven to meet the souls of the blessed, rejoicing with them in the joy of Paradise, and clothing them in robes of splendid glory. As St. Epime looked into the sky that day, he could perceive this happening; he saw the souls of the new martyrs ascending, blessing God and glorifying our Lord Jesus Christ.

After that incident, Epime entered the presence of Armenius, and said to him, "The Lord God almighty lives, the Lord of my soul and my body! You shall not be able to depart from here until you carry out your sentence of death against me, for that is what God has determined." But Armenius could not easily carry out the sentence of death against Epime, because of the crowd of citizens intent upon protecting him. Indeed, all the city loved the saint dearly, on account of the stupendous signs and miracles he had worked in the name of Christ.

Eventually, Armenius resolved upon a course of action. He ordered a lion, a panther and a leopard to be brought to him. These three fierce beasts—together with Epime, whose feet and hands he had bound with rope—he had placed onto a small raft, which was then launched into the sea. As the craft set out upon the ocean waves, the saint sang in a cheerful voice the canticle of the prophet Daniel, in praise of the Lord.

After three days, the archangel Michael led the raft gently to the shore. Now the beasts—the lion, the panther and the leopard—had not harmed the saint in the least; in fact, they were licking him affectionately on the hands and feet. When Armenius saw this, he was astonished, for he had fully expected the wild creatures to have devoured him. But Epime spoke to him, "Be ashamed of yourself, wicked Armenius! For my Lord Jesus Christ has sent His angel, who has kept me safe both from the sea and from these animals, in order that He may confound you and your false idols."

Then Armenius commanded his servants that his tribunal of judgement was to be set up in a maritime location called Posidon, which is close to the sea. He ordered Epime to be attached by chains to a bed of iron,[26] and fire to be applied to him, until he was utterly incinerated. But a shining cloud appeared above the saint and cool rain poured out from it, at once extinguishing the fires. And the iron bed, together with the chains, melted away as if they had been mere wax. So blessed Epime stood again in the presence of Armenius, in perfect health and completely unharmed.

Upon seeing this, Armenius was again filled with unspeakable wrath. But now, a sudden darkness seemed to overtake him, together with all his officers, guards and servants—indeed, they were all rendered completely blind! There was one, however, who remained unaffected. This was Julius the scribe, the same one whose sister had been healed by Epime while he was in prison, and the same one who had pleaded for Epime to heal Armenius earlier, when he had been struck mute.

All the crowd of citizens, perceiving that Epime was unharmed, and utterly astonished at the sudden blindness which had befallen upon Armenius and his court, all shouted with one voice, "Blessed is the Lord God almighty!" Even Armenius himself exclaimed, "Blessed are you, O God of the Christians! Summon to me my faithful officer Julius." And when Julius had come to him, he asked, "What do you advise that I should

---

26 This iron bed was an apparatus to which persons subject to tortures were bound, in order to restrain them.

do? This crowd of citizens will soon rebel against me, and shall surely stone me to death."

Julius turned to Epime, and said to him, "My dear and holy brother, have mercy on us! And let the power of God be once again demonstrated to this crowd." So Epime raised his eyes to Heaven, and prayed. He then went to Armenius and touched his eyes, and then did the same to each of his officers, guards and servants who had been rendered blind. And the darkness immediately departed from their eyes, and their sight was restored.

Armenius though, a prey to insane pride and envy, still felt anger towards the saint and wished to torture him again. But the crowd deeply revered him, and was committed to his protection. "We shall not permit you to harm this good man in any way!" they exclaimed.

Now a domestic manager of the princely palace, Theophanes, and an advisor of the governor, Soterichus, both turned to Armenius, and said to him, "Your Excellency, send this troublesome man away at once into the rural parts of Egypt. Let them kill him there. For if you attempt to torture or kill Epime here in Alexandria once more, the crowd will certainly turn on you with fire and with stones. We well know that the men of this city are of a rebellious nature; and they shall surely not spare any of us!"

Now there was at the time in Alexandria two governors from other provinces, Rhocelianus and Sebastian. Both of these served as governors in provinces of southern Egypt. Having been appointed by Diocletian, they were both strong proponents of the imperial persecution of Christians. Armenius ordered that Epime should be bound hand and foot and a chain placed around his neck, and that he should be handed over to the custody of these two governors. They would then take him away to the rural provinces of the south and kill him there.

Once Epime had been placed aboard the ship to make the voyage south, his friend Julius came to him and embraced him. He said to him, "O my good father! I ask that you remember me wherever you go. May the Lord grant you strength and comfort, until you have completed the martyrdom to which you have been destined." And he called to himself two of his trusted servants, Faustus and Theotimus, and assigned them to St. Epime, that they should minister to him and take care of him, until his earthly life was finished. The two governors, Rhocelianus and Sebastian, both went aboard the ship, and they sailed for the south, to the city of Hnes.[27]

---

27 Modern day Ihnasya el-Medina.

VI

But after voyaging for some time, the winds became unfavorable, and so they all set ashore on the bank near a village known as Phouh Enniameu. There, an angel of the Lord appeared to Epime and touched him on the side, saying to him, "Be ready, O athlete of Christ, your King! For your martyrdom and your crown of glory are now very near. This is the place God has chosen for this purpose, and here your battle for the Faith shall be consummated."

Because of the vehemence of the adverse winds, they were compelled to remain there for three days. The governors then announced to those on board, "There is a temple to the east of the village, dedicated to our gods. Let us arise, and go to pay worship to them!"

One of the governors then ordered oxen to be brought to them, so that they could make the journey to visit this temple. Yet the oxen stood completely still, and could not be induced to move by any means. St. Epime spoke to them, "My Lord Jesus Christ lives! You shall not be permitted to depart from this place, until you have carried out the sentence of death against me. For this is the place which God has chosen for my martyrdom, and my holy destiny must here be fulfilled."

So the governors, seeing that they could travel neither by water nor by land, established their tribunal of judgement there in the village of Phouh Enniameu. They ordered a statue of Apollo to be brought to them from the temple. The governors, together with the soldiers, prostrated themselves before the idol and worshipped. And they commanded that all the Christians who inhabited the area should be brought to them, and be compelled either to worship Apollo, or to die. And a great many were martyred for their Faith.

Now the governor Rhocelianus directed that the statue of Apollo be brought before Epime. He said to him derisively, "This is the true god, the true lord! I have commanded great Apollo to be brought before you, and you shall not be able to perform any of your trickery in his presence!" Epime's heart burned with courage, Faith and righteous indignation. He seized the statue of Apollo and cast it to the ground. He then overturned the throne of the governor from under him, and proclaimed both the emperor and his gods to be wicked and false.

Rhocelianus became utterly enraged. He ordered Epime to be suspended upside down for three hours, until his brains flowed out through his nostrils. After that, he commanded his teeth to be torn out one by one. But the saint felt no pain as he underwent these things.

Next, he directed that a cauldron be brought to him, and in it to be placed a mixture of sulphur, tar and oil. He ordered this to be heated until it was boiling furiously, and then the saint was to be dipped into the mixture with his hands and feet bound. Following this, he commanded that a long needle of iron be heated until it was red hot, and it to be pushed into Epime's right ear, until it should come out through the left!

However, as the soldiers attempted to put this horrendous plan into action, they found themselves thwarted. For once they had cast the saint into the cauldron, flames and sparks lashed out to them, burning and scalding them most severely. Moreover, the saint was seen to rise upwards out of the boiling mixture, without being afflicted by the slightest harm or injury.

Seeing that it was apparently impossible for the soldiers to inflict any pain or harm on Epime, and that all the attempts to torture him were in vain, the governors decided that it would be much better to kill him outright, by simple decapitation.

When they had taken him to the place chosen for his execution, Sebastian ordered that he be brought before him, and spoke to him thus, "Epime, listen to me carefully. You will most surely die. But the choice is yours—whether you die peacefully and easily, or with great pain and disgrace." The saint responded, "When there is a rich man who has sons, the sons always know very well what are the riches possessed by their father. Similarly, I know the riches which are with my God, who dwells in the realms of eternal light! I have directed my heart to Him alone, and I shall soon become a sharer in His Kingdom. The death which I shall die is really no death at all, but everlasting life!"

Rhocelianus responded thus, "Let us be rid of such arrogance and cut off this fellow's head, so that we may have some rest from him. His magical trickery is preventing us from continuing on our journey, and proceeding to our destination."

So the executioners took hold of Epime to carry out his beheading. But he asked them firstly to permit him to spend a little time in prayer before his death, to which they readily agreed. Turning to face the east, St. Epime spoke the following prayer, "My Lord Jesus Christ! Open to me the blessed doors, that I may enter into your Kingdom. O Angels of light and Cherubim, be with me now! Come to me today, O Lord, and be my helper on my journey from this world, until I arrive before the awesome hall of your judgement!"

Having concluded his prayer, the saint turned to the two servants whom Julius had assigned to him, who were standing by, in preparation of attending to his body. He said to them, "Once my head has been cut off, please handle my body with due respect, and place it upon a ship destined for my native village of Pancoleus, that it may be buried in the tomb of my ancestors."

And once he has said this—behold!—the Lord Jesus Christ appeared above him, standing in immense glory, and golden splendor shone forth from him, seven times as radiant as the light of day. The people who were looking on exclaimed, "Look! It is fire from Heaven, sent down to burn us all."

And the Savior then addressed the holy man, "Peace to you, Epime, my chosen one! Be strong and take heart. Do not fear, for I am with you." When the saint had seen the Savior, his heart was filled with indescribable joy, and he fell to the ground and worshipped Him. "My Lord and my God!", said he, "I wish that you will grant me one thing I shall ask of you!" The Lord assured him that He would grant him whatever he asked and bade him to continue with his request, which he did. "I wish that you will give healing and health to all who are sick within my own village, and who come to my tomb and, above my body, invoke Your succor in my name."

The Savior replied, "O Epime, my chosen one! This shall happen not only for those from your own village, but for people from every locality on the earth. For whosoever shall make a pilgrimage to your tomb, venerate your holy body, and pray to Me sincerely in your name, shall be granted health and healing from any affliction. I shall make your name to be revered, and your relics to be venerated, throughout the entire world!"

After this, blessed Epime turned to his executioners, and eagerly asked them to carry out their sentence without delay. This they did, and his holy head was cleanly severed from his body with a single blow. Immediately there flowed forth from his body blood mixed with pure milk.

And the Lord received his soul and embraced it to Himself. He gave to Epime a brilliant, radiant stole, like that of the archangel Michael, and drew him upwards into the highest Heavens. There, God placed upon his head a golden crown of sanctity and perfect bliss, with all the ineffable glory of His eternal Kingdom.

Following Epime's death, the servants of Julius who had been assigned to take care of his body wrapped him carefully in the sheet which their master had given them. They embalmed it with precious spices, and took it by boat to a port close to Pancoleus. There, an angel of the Lord appeared to them, and led them as they completed the remainder of the journey, until they arrived at Pancoleus themselves.

And—behold!—at a certain point, the corpse of the saint opened its mouth and spoke. "Faustus and Theotimus, this is the very place where you must bury me", it said. "This is the place God has chosen for me" And there the servants of Julius buried his body.

When the people of the locality learnt of the saint's resting place, they came to it, to pay their respects with incense, candles, crosses, olive branches and palms. In due course, a splendid church was built there—as was fitting for the resting place of such a noble martyr.

Now I, who write these lines, am the same Julius who has appeared in this narrative. It was my own sister whom he healed; it was I who worked as an official of the wicked prince, Armenius; and it was my own servants who buried the saint. God is my witness, that all I write here is truth, and I have recorded nothing beyond what my own eyes saw and my own ears have heard and my own servants have related to me. It was by the grace of God, and through the actions of St. Epime, that I came to be converted to the true Faith, and to repent of my many sins.

Just as I have narrated, it was thus that the great saint of Christ, blessed Epime, achieved the crown of martyrdom on the eighth day of the month of Epip.[28] On that day, his soul flew upwards to the glorious Kingdom of the Lord Jesus Christ, whom he had loved so dearly during his life. And there he now enjoys infinite and eternal joy, and surely intercedes for all of us sinners below.

My dear brothers and sisters, may we all find mercy and Faith when we face the dreaded tribunal of judgement of the Lord, through the prayers of him whom we now honor, the strong martyr of Christ, St. Epime; in the grace, mercy and humanity of our Lord, God and Savior, Jesus Christ; through whom all glory, honor and adoration is given to the Father, together with the life-giving and consubstantial Holy Spirit, both now and forever. Amen.

---

28 July 15.

THE MARTYRDOM OF
ST. ABANOUB OF NEHISA

by

St. Julius of Aqfahs

The Martyrdom of the St. Abanoub of Nehisa, in the province of Nimesoti, who completed his blessed struggle [for the Faith] on the twenty-fourth day of the month of Epip,[29] in the Peace of God. Amen.

I

It came to pass during the reign of the emperor Diocletian[30] that the devil caused his heart to stray from the God of Heaven, so that he came to worship gods made by human hands. Diocletian established Armenius as prince of Alexandria. He sent to every place in Egypt governors, leaders, eparchs, military commanders and soldiers—from Rumania to Philae, which lies beyond the borders of Egypt—commanding that these should put to death all Christians. And Diocletian, the wicked emperor, made for himself seventy idols, representing all of the pagan gods. And he declared them to be deities, although they were not truly gods at all, but merely works of art. Thirty-five were males and thirty-five were females. Amongst them, Apollo held primacy of place, followed by Jupiter and Artemis, then all the others [in due order].

Furthermore, he commanded all the populace to offer sacrifice to these idols and all Christian churches to be destroyed in every location. And he issued an edict to all territories which were under his power, which read thus:

> *I, the Emperor Diocletian, send forth this edict*
> *to all lands and peoples within my empire. At*
> *whatever time this edict reaches you and you read*
> *it—whether you be a prince, or a governor, or a*
> *military commander, or an eparch, or a noble, or*

---

29 July 31.
30 284-305 AD.

a tribune, or a soldier, or a pagan, or a bishop or priest or deacon or sub-deacon or reader or singer of psalms or a monk or a lay person, or a man or a woman, or one of the little or one of the great— the same command applies to you all! You are to worship the gods which I have established, namely Apollo, Jove and Artemis, the honored mother of all the gods. Regarding those who fail to obey this edict, authority is hereby given to you to subject them to tortures, in whatever manner you please. After this [if they do not comply with this edict], you are to behead them with a sword and have their bodies incinerated in fire, so that no trace at all of them shall remain.

Once the emperor Diocletian had written this edict he promulgated it throughout the entire globe, in a state of great fury and diabolical rage. And when the edict arrived at Alexandria, it was given to the prince of that great metropolis, Armenius. When he received it, he kissed it respectfully. He then commanded a herald to proclaim throughout all the city that all were to assemble together before his palace. Once this was done, he read the edict aloud. And great turmoil arose in the city. Many offered sacrifice to the gods in accordance with the edict, so that the air itself was darkened with the smoke of the multitude of burnt offerings. But many declared themselves to be Christians and so were slaughtered, thus accepting the imperishable crown of holy martyrdom.

[Now, there was a certain military commander, by the name of Euhios.] When this Euhios received a copy of the edict of

Diocletian, he went to the city of Athribis[31] and saw Cyprian, the governor of that city. He handed governor Cyprian a copy of the edict, who read it for himself. Then they both went into the temple and offered worship to Apollo and to Artemis, and passed the whole of the night, [merrily] eating and drinking together. The next morning they arrested many Christians and cast them into the city prison, on account of their allegiance to the Name of Christ. Amongst those whom they arrested was a certain handsome young man, of twenty years of age. His name was Sergius, and he was the son of a scholar called Theodore, who was the brother of Cyprian, the governor of Athribis.[32] [Despite being his own nephew], the godless and cruel Cyprian subjected [Sergius] to severe tortures, for the sake of his Faith in the Name of Jesus Christ.

Others who were subject to torture included the priests Apa Meneson and his brother [who was also a priest], Apa Plou. There was also Paesi and his brothers, as well as George, John, Isidore, Pisoi, Apa Cragon, Sarapamone, Zacharia, Pithos, Macarius, Jacob, Turoda, Apollo, Amun, Dioscorus, and many others whom we are not able to name here. When they had finished torturing these men, they bound them in irons, and cast them into prison because of their fidelity to the name of Christ. There were altogether some 850 persons who refused to sacrifice to the pagan gods. The governor, Cyprian, and the military commander, Euhios, deliberated carefully about what they should do with all these prisoners.

Now, there was a certain man, Macarius by name, in the village of Nehisa in the province of Nimesoti. He was a devout lover of God, and also lover of charity and a lover of the Church. The

---

31 Modern day Tell Atrib.

32 The significance of this detail seems to be to show the ruthlessness of the governor, in being prepared to have his own nephew made subject to torture.

name of his wife was Maria. They lived in the love and blessing of God, and God loved them for their devotion and innocence of life. They had an only son, and apart from him had no other offspring. His parents loved their son very much and held him dearer than their own lives.

Now it happened that this boy's father, Macarius, passed away; and, after a few days, his mother, Maria, died as well. The youth mourned and wept for them sincerely for some time. The youth's name was Abanoub. He was very handsome, humble, meek, modest and virtuous. He was at this time twelve years old.

On a certain day of one of the Christian solemnities, when the sacred rites were celebrated in the Church, the boy accepted the sacrament of the Holy Eucharist. And the priest addressed the congregation and told them, "My brothers and sisters, we have all heard how the devil has arisen against the Church, in an attempt to abolish true religion and the worship of the Body and Blood of our Lord Jesus Christ! Therefore, all of you who hear me today, I urge you to be steadfast and patient in the orthodox Faith and in the gift of baptism which you have received. Do not let the false words of the enemies of truth deceive you, and never deny the sweet Name of our Lord Jesus Christ! Have no fear of passing torments. Do not let the fleeting glories of this world deprive you of the eternal glories of the Kingdom of Heaven. Do not fear the fires of this world; lest the eternal fire of Gehenna, the worm which does not die, and the agonized grinding of teeth should overtake you! My children, know that this will surely be the last day on which we celebrate these sacred mysteries together, [for the persecutors of the Church are soon to attack us.] Therefore, all you who hear me now, know that those who, by suffering martyrdom, receive the crown of victory in Heaven are most truly blessed!" When the elderly priest had said these things and dismissed the congregation with the sign of peace, they all returned to their homes with a great sadness in their hearts, because of the great storm which had arisen against all those who held the Christian Faith.

The youth Abanoub required for himself very little of the wealth of his parents which they had bequeathed to him. Indeed, they had been very rich. But the boy took no food or drink beyond that which he received in the sacrament of the Holy Eucharist. He collected before him all the gold and precious garments which were in his house. Looking upon these riches, he said, "It is written, 'Gold decays, silver becomes corroded and vestments are consumed by worms.'[33] And Scripture also says, 'The world and the desires thereof, and all that is contained therein, shall pass away. But the one who does the will of God shall live forever'.[34]"

Then he took all that he had that was of value, and distributed it as alms to the poor and needy of the city. He arose and went forth through the doorway of his house. Extending his hands, he turned his face to the east and prayed;

> *"My Lord Jesus Christ, Son of the living God! Just as I have now walked through this open doorway, and as I have walked after you in my heart, lead me now to the palace of the governor.*
>
> *And send to me your angel of light, that he may stand by my side and strengthen me to endure the tortures of the persecution. My Lord Jesus Christ, send to me the archangel Michael, that he may accompany me to the governor's presence, and grant me bold speech so that I may proclaim Your truth in the presence of the kings and governors.*

---

33 Cf. James 5:2-3.
34 1 John 2:17.

For yours is the glory for ever and ever, together with your Heavenly Father and the Holy Spirit. Amen."

When he had proclaimed this prayer, he walked by himself to the south, along the side of the river, till he arrived at Gemnuti. Entering the town, he found all the Christian Churches to have been overturned, and temples dedicated to idols raised in the places. Suddenly, he began to feel apprehensive. Walking through the city, he overheard various people speaking against our Lord Jesus Christ, even people who had formerly worshipped Him. He enquired of some locals as to the name of the governor of the city. They indicated to him [the palace of the governor, and told him that his name was Lysias. He waited for the remainder of the day. But when evening had fallen, he raised his hands and prayed:

> *"O, forgiving and patient God, Your mercies are truly many!*
>
> *O, just God, You accept to Yourself sinners, of whom I am the first.*
>
> *You made your angel go ahead of the three Magi, so that they could bear to You their gifts.*
>
> *You heard the prophet Elijah, and sent fire down from Heaven for him.*
>
> *You heard the pleadings of our ancestor Adam, and led him back to paradise.*
>
> *O Lord, hear my prayer now, and send to me the angel of Your light, that he may give me strength to endure, even unto the shedding of my blood!"*

While St. Abanoub was still praying, behold, the archangel Michael descended from the sky. The whole place shone with the radiance and gleaming splendor of the noontide sun. The youth at once fell upon his face [in awe and surprise], and became like one who is dead. But Michael touched him and raised him up to his feet, saying, "Greetings, good youth, Abanoub, and greetings from God! O noble man, be strong and take courage. I am Michael, the commander of the Heavenly army. The Lord has sent me to strengthen you in the battle which you shall undergo. Tomorrow, when you awaken, go straight to the governor and proclaim to him the Name of Christ. For three days you shall be subject to tortures, but I shall strengthen you and heal your body. And then they shall lead you to the south to Athribis,[35] and torture you there. But you shall confound Satan and all of his wicked demons! I shall be with you in every place to which you go." Once he had said this, the archangel Michael made to Abanoub a sign of peace and ascended upwards to the Heaven in his glory, while the saint looked on.

---

35 Modern day Tell Atrib.

II

When the light of morning appeared, Abanoub arose and went forth to see the governor. He found that he had set up his tribunal of judgement before the door of a temple. Before had had been asked any question, he cried out boldly in a loud voice, "O, governor Lysias! I believe in my Lord Jesus Christ! Do to me what you please and do it quickly, for I shall never worship your impure idols!"

The governor was astonished at these words and said to him, "Where have you come from, you unknown youth? Or who has brought you here? Indeed, the sun has hardly risen yet." St. Abanoub responded, "O, you godless governor! How foolish are both you and your [false god,] Apollo! I have heard that you speak against my Lord Jesus Christ and kill those who worship Him. I have left my own land and come here and am fully ready to pour out my blood for the holy Name of my Lord Jesus Christ, who alone made the earth and the sea and all that is contained therein. He created humanity in His own image, and created the birds and beast and reptiles as well. But your Apollo is deaf, blind and lifeless. He does not have the power even to save himself, much less to save others! Do to me whatever you like, but I shall never adore your detestable gods."

[Perplexed,] the governor asked him, "But where do you come from? And what is your name, that you should speak thus without reserve and without fear?" Abanoub, that noble warrior of Christ, answered thus, "You godless wretch, hear me and I shall reveal to you from whence I am come. I am of the village of Nehisa in the province of Nimesoti. My name is Abanoub, or at least that is the name my parents gave me. But now that I have come here, my name is 'The Servant of Christ'! Behold, I am prepared to undergo any tortures for the One who strengthens me, Christ. Woe to you, you wretched villain! And woe to all, who worship your idols! Woe to the stumbling block, and woe to the one through who such a stumbling block has come[36]— that is, to you and your godless superiors, and the idols, and all who worship them!"

Upon hearing this, the governor was infuriated. He said to him, "I see that you are a handsome and delicate person, and only a youth. Therefore, you will scarcely be able to sustain any torture at all. If I struck you once, I would not need to strike you a second time! But if you obey me, I shall make you my own son[-in-law.] I shall promote you to greatness amongst my eparchs, and many shall honor you on account of what I shall do for you. If you give proper worship to the great god Apollo, I shall give you [my own daughter] as your wife!"[37]

But the saint answered, "May my Lord Jesus Christ curse you, together with your insensate, stone Apollo!" The governor was enraged and ordered Abanoub to be seized. He had him thrown down upon his back. Four torturers, two alternating with two, then set upon him with blows and scourges, until his innards

---

36   Matthew 18:7.

37   This offer of marriage to his daughter on the part of governor Lysias seems to have been made on account of Abanoub's handsome appearance, although this is not entirely clear.

flowed out and all the bones in his chest were shattered. The blessed youth gave out a tremendous cry, saying,

> *"Hear me, my Lord Jesus Christ, for You are the eye that sees and the ear that hears! You came into the world and took upon Yourself our sufferings for the salvation of the human race.*
>
> *You who are immortal and incorruptible accepted death. Indeed, You tasted death for our sake and because of our sins. But You arose strongly, like a mighty warrior arising after drinking wine.*[38]
>
> *Hear me, my Lord, who am undergoing these pains for the sake of Your glorious name. For all glory is Yours alone, together with Your Heavenly Father and the Holy Spirit, for ever and ever. Amen."*

Just as he uttered the "Amen" in conclusion of his prayer, behold, the blessed archangel Michael descended from Heaven! He carried a splendid crown in his hand, and said to the righteous youth Abanoub, "Take comfort and be strong, O beloved of God! You have taken up your cross and willingly followed your Lord. I am the archangel Michael, who stand at the right hand of God almighty. It is I who strengthen the martyrs, so that they receive their crown of victory. I am the one who gives endurance to all the just, and to all holy hermits so that they may sustain their manner of life. Look! You see in my hands a splendid crown, which I shall place upon your head!" And immediately he raised his hands over the saint's body. He entirely healed him of his injuries, and restored his scattered innards to his abdomen. After this, the archangel returned to the Heavens in peace and glory.

---

38 Psalm 78:65.

Then, strengthened by the power of Christ, St. Abanoub arose and went straight to the governor. He spoke to him boldly, saying, "O wicked tyrant! What do you have to say to me now? Behold, my Lord Jesus Christ has healed me from all your cruel tortures which you attempted to inflict upon me. Do whatever you please to me, for I shall never, ever worship your abominable idols!"

The governor turned to his nobles and said to them, "Come! See this youth, who has employed the magic arts of the Christians. Woe to this wretch! For now his handsome appearance shall be totally destroyed by tortures, and his Jesus will not be able to save him from my hands."

[Now, at that time the governor had to make a journey to the south.] So he ordered Abanoub to be cast into a dungeon, until he had been to the south and returned. Abanoub, having been placed in prison, found that there were a number of men who were being held there because of their Faith in Christ. He spoke to them, saying, "My brothers, arise! Let us all go to this wretched governor and show our disdain for his polluted idols! Perhaps he will torture us. In that case, we shall indeed receive some sufferings for the sake of our Lord Jesus Christ, but in return shall be rewarded with an imperishable crown in the Kingdom of the Heavens!"

[Encouraged by these words,] all the prisoners arose as a group and proceeded to the gates of the prison. From there, they saw that the governor was about to board a boat in order to sail to the south, with his whole army accompanying him on other boats. Indeed, the governor was planning on going to the city of Athribis, to see there Cyprian, the governor of that city, and Euhios, the military commander. But the prisoners called out to him in a loud voice, demanding of him, "As Christ, our God lives, we shall not permit you to travel to the south until you pass your sentence of death upon us! May you be burnt up, together with your idol of Apollo made of stone, your other filthy idols, and Diocletian, your wicked and accursed emperor!"

At this the governor was filled with fear, hearing the great clamor of the multitude. He therefore abandoned his boat and set up his tribunal of judgement to hear the cases of all those who were detained for their Faith. News of this development immediately spread throughout the whole multitude of Christians held in the prison. [By sheer force of numbers,] they forced themselves out, and the whole city was filled with the outcry: "We are Christians! We proclaim this openly. There is no God in Heaven nor on earth apart from our Lord Jesus Christ! He will destroy all the filthy idols of the pagans."

When the governor saw what was happening he was greatly perturbed. He ordered all the multitude of Christians to be put to the sword, from the third hour of the day until the ninth hour.[39] Thus the blood of these martyrs flowed through the streets and squares. They were all beheaded—men and women, great and small—for the sake of the name of Christ. Those killed were some 8,000 souls. Each of these accepted as reward for their noble martyrdom an imperishable crown of splendor, on the ninth day of the month of Phamenoth.[40]

[After this had been done,] the governor said to his ministers, "Now we may have some respite from the clamor of this toxic crowd! Let us now go forth to the city of Athribis, as we had planned, and see the governor, Cyprian, and Euhios, the military commander." At this, one of his soldiers told him, "O lord and governor, there is still a certain youth who remained in the prison. Since he was bound in iron fetters he was not able

---

39 That is, from nine o'clock in the morning until three o'clock in the afternoon.

40 March 18.

to escape with the rest of the multitude whom you killed. But it was he who stirred up all the crowd of rioters that have been put to death. I suggest, therefore, that you should have him brought before you, so that you may know what is in his heart." And so Abanoub was brought before the governor by his troops, barely able to walk because of all the heavy iron chains in which he was bound.

When he was before the tribunal of judgement, the governor said to him, "You madman! You came into this city, and because of you there has been much death and slaughter amongst its inhabitants. Even those who had previously obeyed me and given due honor to the imperial gods have now risen up against me, all because of your influence. I have been compelled to kills huge numbers of citizens, all because of you! But now I say to you; obey me! Come and sacrifice to the glorious gods, according to the mandate of the noble emperor."

But immediately, blessed Abanoub picked up off the ground with both hands a huge lump of manure, and hurled it into the face of the governor! As he did so he exclaimed, "You rabid dog! From the third hour of this day until now, I have seen the angels of the Lord in the air, placing crowns upon the heads of all those whom you have cruelly martyred this day. Hurry up, I say! Do to me whatever you please. I have my Lord Jesus Christ as my protector and guardian, who will bring to naught your wickedness and protect me from all ill."

Upon hearing this the governor was infuriated. He commanded that Abanoub should be suspended from the mast of the ship, which was in readiness for his voyage to the south. He said, "By the great god Apollo, and by Artemis, the blessed mother of the gods, this wretch shall remain suspended from the mast until we arrive at Athribis. Then we shall see whether or not this Jesus of Nazareth is able to save him!"

III

And so blessed Abanoub was suspended from the mast of the ship, while the governor and all his troops went on board. They sailed southwards throughout the whole day until evening fell. At that time the sails were lowered and the governor prepared himself to take his meal. But as he attempted to drink from his goblet, the wine solidified and became like stone. His arm likewise became stiff, as if it had been turned to stone, and he was entirely unable to bend or to move it. All of his soldiers were suddenly overcome by darkness and made blind so that they were totally unable to perceive anything of the light.

At this the wicked governor was overcome with fear. He raised his eyes to look upon St. Abanoub and saw the blessed youth suspended from the mast, with blood flowing forth from his nostrils and mouth. But immediately Lysias saw the holy archangel Michael appear in all his glory. He touched the youth with his hand and washed away the blood which oozed from his mouth and nose. And Michael unbound the ropes which held him and placed him upon the deck of the ship [showing no sign of injury at all]. The governor exclaimed desperately, "O Abanoub, I now believe in you! You are indeed the servant of the Lord Jesus Christ. If you heal me now, O Abanoub, I and all my soldiers shall become Christians. I have witnessed the great glory and power of your God today with my own eyes. I do not need anyone else to tell me these things, for I have seen them myself."

Abanoub replied to him, "Truly my God lives, the Lord Jesus Christ, the King of Heaven and earth! You are not able to be saved until you and all your soldiers arrive at the city of Athribis, so that all who reside there may come to know that there is no other God apart from my Lord Jesus Christ." Upon hearing this, the soldiers [who had been rendered blind] all cried out together, "We all proclaim ourselves openly to be Christians now! We place our faith entirely in the God of St. Abanoub of Nehisa."

At this, a strong wind arose and impelled the ship to the city of Athribis in a short time. But the governor, [who had been paralyzed,] was unable to stand up or to walk, in order to disembark from the ship. However, the soldiers, [still blinded,] left the ship and, [guided by touch alone,] made their way to the tetrapylon[41] of the city. They found there a tribunal of judgement to be set up, where the governor, Cyprian, and the military commander, Euhios, were in the process of having Christians executed.

All of the soldiers [who had been converted to the Christian Faith whilst on the ship] removed their belts of military service and threw them in the face of Cyprian. They declared, "We are Christians now! We place our hopes in the Faith in which St. Abanoub believes." Cyprian enquired, "Who is this Abanoub?! And why have you come here? Why have you left your own city?" The soldiers replied, "[Our own governor, Lysias, has been struck with paralysis. And his god, Apollo, has not been able to

---

41 A place of public assembly, consisting of four large pillars with a roof on top.

cure him from his plight.] If this Apollo is not capable of healing him, why should we place our faith in him?"

Curious, the governor Cyprian enquired, "And where is your governor at the moment?" They replied, "He is still on the boat, for he had attempted to injure the servant of Christ, St. Abanoub, and so has been paralyzed and is unable to walk. As for ourselves, we also were punished by being made blind. In fact, we still cannot see anything and only made our way here by feeling with our hands!" Upon hearing this Cyprian ordered that Lysias be carried off the ship and taken to him. Five men carried him and placed him in the presence of Cyprian and his tribunal.

Euhios, the military commander, then questioned him, "Which one of the Christians is it who has performed such wizardry against you, to place you in the condition of paralysis?" Lysias answered him, "It is a certain youth who is quite unknown, but bears the name of Abanoub. I have dealt with many Christians before, but never once did I encounter any who are like this one!" The tribunal then ordered Abanoub to be brought before him.

When he arrived, he was suffused with all the power that the archangel Michael had imparted to him. His face shone with the splendor of the sun, while his eyes glowed like the stars of the morning. His whole countenance radiated strength and life, like one who has just arisen from a wonderful feast.

The governor Cyprian said to him, "What is your name, young man?" The saint replied, "My name is Abanoub, and I am the servant of Christ, my Lord. I have come here so that I may pour out my blood for the sake of His blessed Name. And I have come here so that I may confound you and your detestable idols. Indeed, these lifeless deities have no power to save themselves, much less anyone else!"

Cyprian, flushed with anger, replied to him, "You are a mere worker of magical tricks! You should know that you are no longer in Gemnuti. We have here much greater and much more dreadful methods of torture! Obey me and sacrifice to the gods lest you come to die a terrible death at my hands." But the saint answered him with calm reassurance, "God forbid that I should ever do what you say, O wretched scoundrel, and abandon my Lord Jesus Christ to worship your worthless idols! You are completely godless, together with your fiendish emperor, Diocletian!"

The governor was infuriated at this defiance. He commanded that Abanoub should be stripped naked, then flogged a hundred times with a whip fashioned from the sinews of an ox. After this, he had him chained to a bed of iron. Then he had a blazing fire lit underneath the saint, fueled with sulphur and with pitch, until its flames reached upwards for some twelve feet.

While this was happening, the blessed youth prayed calmly,

> *"Blessed are you, Lord God of our fathers, and exalted and worthy of all praise is Your name forever and ever!*[42]
>
> *My Lord Jesus Christ, my helper, hear me as I cry out to You from this fire! Amen. Alleluia!*
>
> *My Lord Jesus Christ, my true light, listen to my pleadings from the midst of these flames! Amen. Alleluia! My Lord Jesus Christ, my hope and my protector, save me, Your humble servant. Amen. Alleluia!*

---

42 1 Chronicles 29:10.

My Lord Jesus Christ, my liberator, come quickly to me! Help me, who am surrounded by this pack of ravenous wolves! And by doing this, let this crowd behold Your immense power, and give glory to Your holy name. For Yours indeed is the glory, together with Your Heavenly Father, and the Holy Spirit, both now and forever. Amen."

As Abanoub uttered the concluding "Amen" of this prayer, behold, the Lord Jesus Christ came to him, mounted upon a fiery chariot. To His right stood the archangel Michael, while to His left was Gabriel.

The Lord spoke thus to Abanoub,

"My beloved and holy Abanoub! Be strong and have no fear. I am the Lord, and I am with you. Do not be discouraged!

Behold, I appoint my archangel Michael as your guardian, and he shall strengthen you.

I am Jesus, your King, and it is for My holy Name that you suffer these things.

I tell you that, through you, a certain governor will become a martyr, and many other souls along with him.

"You shall be tortured in two locations. But blessed Michael will stand by your side and shall give you fortitude. No harm shall overcome you. You shall eventually be sent to Alexandria, and it is there you shall complete the glorious struggle

of your martyrdom. But I shall appoint Julius of Aqfahs, the scribe, so that he shall return your mortal remains to your home province, and there honorably bury your body.

"I swear by My own self and by My blessed angels, whoever venerates your body or honors it shall be honored by Me in My eternal Kingdom. And whoever recalls the narrative of your blessed martyrdom or commits it to writing, or employs a scribe to make a copy of it—his name shall be inscribed by Me in the Book of Life, and, if he has committed any sins, these shall be forgiven him. If anyone gives food to the hungry or alms to the poor in honor of you, and the day of your commemoration, I—whom am God almighty— shall reward him with a splendid Heavenly banquet, which shall last one thousand years. And if anyone should clothe the naked in your name, I—who am the omnipotent Deity—shall erase all record of his sins, be they murder, fornication, false oaths or theft—in one word, any sin whatsoever! And I shall do this on account of your sacrifice and sanctity."

And the Lord then directed the archangel Michael, who preserved Abanoub from all harm. Indeed, he made the flames around him become as mild as cool water. The Savior extended his hands over the saint and healed all his wounds, restored him to perfect health, and imparted to him His own strength. And Abanoub said to the Savior, "My Lord and my God! I humbly request that You command my body to be taken to my native province, to the land of my ancestors, when I have passed from this life." And Christ reassured him that whatever he asked of Him would surely be granted. After this, the Savior made the sign of the cross over the saint, and covered him with refreshing and cool dew. He then ascended into the Heavens, suffused with radiant glory.

IV

St. Abanoub arose from the fire [completely unharmed], and boldly proceeded once more to the tetrapylon. He found there Cyprian the governor, Euhios the military commander and Lysias, the governor of Gemnuti. There was also an imperial emissary, Marcellus. He had with him a new edict from the emperor Diocletian, as well as many troops. The saint found them there reading the edict of Diocletian, the text of which was:

Be alert! Remain watchful! Do not permit anyone under the entire firmament of Heaven to utter the name of Jesus or to give Him veneration or worship! Give all glory to Apollo, to Jupiter, to Athena and to Artemis! Let all the earth adore these deities, for it is they who have given glorious military victories into my hands. And whatever fraudster, magician or wizard refuses to obey you on this matter—have him sent to Alexandria. There, the noble prince Armenius shall put them to death without mercy!

Abanoub waited patiently until this edict had been read. But then, filled with the power of God, he leapt into the air and seized the edict from the hands of the governors. He tore it into pieces and then hurled the fragments into their faces, exclaiming, "Be confounded, you godless scoundrels, together with your deaf and dumb Apollo! Why do you refer to the servants of Christ as 'magicians'? We are certainly nothing like that! But you yourselves saw the punishments which you tried to inflict upon me. And, behold, my Lord Jesus Christ has come to my assistance! He has imparted to me his strength and healing, so that I should disgrace and thwart you and all your hateful idols!"

At this, the governor Cyprian was inflamed with black rage and ground his teeth at Abanoub. He snarled, "You evil trickster! How are you able to appear before me again? By the great god Apollo, and by the mother of all the gods, Artemis, none of the Christians has been able to annoy me in this way, except for this confounded youth, who is nothing but a venomous and deceitful wizard!"

He then commanded that an iron bench be brought in and the saint to be bound to it, while a fire was lit under him. Then he ordered that two metal spikes, made red hot from fire, should be driven into his eyes and twisted around violently, until his eyeballs spilled out to the ground!

As this was done, blessed Abanoub exclaimed, "I give thanks to You, my Lord Jesus Christ! This wretched governor has now freed me from the sight of him! He has relieved me of seeing his hideous looks, too—and his horrid stare of low cunning, which is filled with the evil gaze of Satan, and with perverse and effeminate lusts."[43]

---

43 The implication here seems to be that Cyprian exhibited a homosexual or pedophilic attraction to Abanoub.

After this, the governor ordered a double wheel made of heavy iron with sharp serrated teeth to be brought in. This he ordered to be rolled over the saint repeatedly, until his body was divided into three separate pieces; one part from his chest upwards, the other part, his abdomen, and the third part his legs and feet. As this was being done, the saint cried out in prayer, "Hear me, my Lord Jesus Christ! Hear me, for You are the ear that hears the cry of those in need, and You are the all-seeing eye which looks with pity and judgement. And Yours is the glory for all eternity. Amen."

When he had concluded his prayer, behold, the archangel Michael descended from Heaven. He shattered the iron wheel into pieces, and took the severed portions of the saint's body and joined them together once more. He collected also his eyeballs, which had spilt to the ground, and restored them to their right places in their socket, healing them as he did so. Finally, he raised the youth to his feet, so that he stood upright, displaying perfect health and well-being. The angel then said, "Take courage, holy Abanoub, and be strong! I will be with you throughout all your sufferings and I shall impart to you my fortitude and endurance. You shall accept as a reward an imperishable crown of glory, and a great multitude shall come to believe in Christ through you." Having said this, he ascended once more into Heaven, in a blaze of light.

Thus the blessed Abanoub rose up from all his tortures, entirely free from injury and infused with Divine strength. And an entire crowd witnessed this with wonder. A vast multitude of the citizens of Athribis proclaimed, "We are now Christians, and we openly declare ourselves to be such! We belong to the God in whom St. Abanoub has placed his Faith!"

Now a certain Magmentius, the governor of Thmuis,[44] was also present at the time and had witnessed all that had taken place. At

---

44 Modern day Tell el-Timai.

this point he leapt up and tore his garments. He took his sandals from his feet and placed them mockingly upon the heads of the governors Cyprian and Lysias, saying to them, "Your eyes are blinded by the madness of your father, the devil![45] Can you not see clearly the power and glory which Jesus gives to His martyrs? It is on account of this manifest and undeniable evidence of His power and grace that I also declare myself to be a Christian, along with all this multitude. Let the idols be destroyed, along with all who worship them!"

When Cyprian and Lysias saw the great disturbances which had arisen in the city they commanded their troops to go forth and put to death at the edge of the sword all those who confessed themselves to be Christians. They waged their bloody slaughter the whole day, mercilessly wielding their swords from dawn until evening. Some 885 were killed, who poured forth their blood in noble martyrdom for the holy Name of our Lord Jesus Christ, on the eight day of the month of Pashons[46] in the peace of God. Amen. And all the while, St. Abanoub encouraged and comforted them with his prayers and exhortations, until, as holy martyrs, they each received their imperishable crown of glory in the eternal bliss of Heaven.

The military commander, Euhios, spoke to the righteous Abanoub, saying, "O Abanoub of Nehisa, won't you be persuaded to sacrifice to the official gods? You have seen today much innocent blood poured out. And the fault is entirely yours. Worst of all, you have caused even one of the governors, noble Magmentius, to fall into this error. Leave behind your empty and foolish words! Come and simply offer the customary worship of Apollo, in accordance with the decree of our lord, Diocletian." But Abanoub retorted, "Diocletian may be *your*

---

45 Cf. John 8:44.

46 May 16.

lord, but he is certainly not *my* Lord! My Lord is Jesus Christ, who is Lord not only of earth, but of Heaven too. It is He who lowers and He who exalts. And He shall indeed humiliate all the proud and haughty—those who are like you and like your father, the devil!" [47]

When he heard this, Euhios was filled with uncontrollable wrath. He ordered a sharp, double-edged sword to be brought in. He had Abanoub thrown down on the ground on his back. Then he commanded his troops to amputate both of the saint's legs, from the knees, and both of his arms, from the elbows. When this cruel and inhuman deed was done, the youth was left lying on the ground, close to death. Meanwhile Euhios stood by, [proudly and arrogantly.] He boasted, "By the great god Apollo! I have triumphed over this wretched and guilty youth. Let his Jesus, the Galilean, come now and rescue him from my hands, if He can! For in truth, there is no god except for great Apollo and Artemis!"

When the crowds saw what had happened and looked upon Abanoub lying there, as if he were dead, they were filled with deepest mourning and sorrow. "Alas, the saint is dead", they wailed. The governor, Cyprian, was filled with evil joy, and ordered his dogs to be brought, so that they could devour the body of Abanoub. He had no relatives of friends in that town to keep watch and prayer over his body, except for a certain pious youth of the city, by the name of Apoli.

Suddenly, the archangel Michael came down from Heaven, accompanied by Suriel and Raphael! These took up the saint's severed members and restored them to his body, miraculously healing his wounds and giving soundness to his flesh and bones. Next, the angelic beings breathed into the face of the saint,

---

47 Cf. John 8:44.

and—behold!—he rose to his feet, filled with life and free from any harm or injury.

Suriel then spoke to him, "Be strong and take courage, for you are an athlete of Christ and noble hero of the Faith! We shall be with you throughout all your struggles, bestowing upon you endurance and fortitude. And you shall confound the guilty wretch who has done this thing to you and put to shame all his filthy idols! Know that they will take you to the city of Alexandria, to the prince Armenius. He will torture you; but we shall come to you and shall heal you. Afterwards, Armenius will pass the sentence of death upon you and have you decapitated. But Julius of Aqfahs will return your body to your home province and entomb you honorably and reverently there. Many healings shall take place in the location in which your mortal remains shall rest. Indeed, the Lord shall bestow his blessings upon that place until the end of the age. Whoever goes there suffering from some infirmity, if they venerate your holy body, shall be cured. But if anyone makes a false oath over your tomb or speaks vain or impious things there, we shall punish him with due retribution; such a person will be reduced to a state of poverty for all eternity." Once they had said all these things to St. Abanoub, the holy angels Michael, Suriel and Raphael departed again into the splendor of the Heavens.

Abanoub was greatly encouraged, and proceeded to make his way to the city prison. A great multitude followed him, comprising men and women, young and old, small and great alike. And they all shouted in unison as they went, "There is no deity in Heaven nor on earth, except for the God whom St. Abanoub, the blessed martyr of Christ has proclaimed!" The news of this soon came to the ears of the arrogant and wicked governors, Cyprian and Lysias. Lysias observed, "This troublesome youth, Abanoub, has now arrived at the prison with a great multitude. He is curing the sick, giving sight to the blind, casting out demons, giving speech to the mute, cleansing lepers, and making the lame to walk!"

Cyprian was bewildered, and asked, "Didn't the dogs, the crows and the vultures devour his body? What shall we do with this accursed magician? He has confounded us greatly already, and has incited the whole populace of the city to rebellion against our authority!"

Lysias and Euhios both reminded Cyprian of the imperial edict of Diocletian, which directed all Christians who refused to renounce their Faith and to worship the official idols to be sent to Armenius, the prince of Alexandria, to be put to death there. They recommended to him, "Let us send this wizard Abanoub to Alexandria, and entrust him to the custody of Armenius. In this way, we can escape from his trickery and the unrest which he is generating throughout the whole city." Cyprian replied, "Indeed! You have certainly suggested the most prudent course of action. By this means, we will have some rest from this wretch, who spurns the powers of the divinities themselves!"

Immediately they sent troops to the entrance of the prison to arrest Abanoub, where he and the crowd which accompanied him had congregated. As they did so, the whole assembly cried out, "If Abanoub dies for the sake of Christ, we also wish to die for Him!"

At this, the governors realized that they were utterly powerless to take any further action against him, on account of the unrest of the people. Resigning themselves to this, they sat down and composed the following letter:

> *We, Cyprian and Lysias, governors of Athribis and Gemnuti respectively, and Euhios, the military commander, write this letter to our noble lord, Armenius, the prince of Alexandria. Hail! It is our*

resolve to act in accordance with the edict of our lord the emperor, Diocletian, who has mandated that all the world should worship and adore Apollo and Artemis. A certain Christian youth by the name of Abanoub, from the province of Nimesoti, has come to our attention. He is an infamous practitioner of the magical arts. Indeed, there is no wizard or trickster amongst all the Christians like him—except perhaps for Victor, the son of Romanus. He has incited a great multitude to rebellion and defiance against us, and it has been necessary for us to execute a great number of persons. We are concerned lest civil war should break out on account of the influence of this Abanoub. Therefore, in pursuance to the imperial edict, we send him to you. Dispose of him as you will, for we are unable to prevail against him, or to induce him to comply with the decree of the Emperor. May the great gods grant you health and prosperity!

Having affixed their signatures to this brief letter, they gave it to their troops. Abanoub was bound in heavy iron chains, weighing about one hundred pounds, on his hands and feet. But when the troops, under the direction of the governors, attempted to put the saint on board a ship to sail to Alexandria, and enormous crowd of people assembled by the river, and forcibly obstructed them from doing so. "We shall not permit you to take Abanoub away, unless you kill us!" they shouted. Upon hearing this, the wicked governors were filled with fear. They ordered their troops to draw their swords, and to put to death anyone who offered resistance, man or woman, old or young, servant or freeborn.

This they did, and the blood flowed forth as a veritable torrent, swirling everywhere as a crimson waterfall, and soaking the earth with gore. They hurled others into the river. The bodies of the dead and the dying were strewn on the ground everywhere. All the while Abanoub stood by, offering words of encouragement and exhortation to embrace holy martyrdom. "Be strong and have courage," he exclaimed, "and you shall be made worthy of the celestial Kingdom of Heaven!" And as these brave martyrs gave up their souls—behold!—angels of light placed upon the heads of each one a crown. Those who were martyred on this fateful day numbered one thousand men and eighty-two women. Thus they accepted their well-deserved crowns of imperishable glory, on the tenth day of the month of Paoni.[48]

---

48 June 17.

V

The troops now placed Abanoub upon the ship bound for Alexandria, and they all began to sail towards the south. As they departed from the shore, the saint prayed thus:

> "I give thanks to you, my Lord Jesus Christ, for you have given rest to my spirit. Lord, I have beheld your angels placing splendid crowns upon the heads of those who were martyred for the sake of Your holy Name. Grant to me strength, O Christ, so that Your will for me may be fulfilled. You know that I am a pilgrim and an exile, far from my native province. I have neither kith nor kin to comfort me. My father and mother have left this world and there is no relative or compatriot who will take my body and my bones to my home province as their resting place. But you, my Lord Jesus Christ, are both my brother and sister. You are my protector and refuge. I place my hope in You alone. Do not desert me, my Lord and my God!"

And he continued to pray in this way, not ceasing until the middle of the night.

At that time, the archangel Michael appeared to him in the hull of the ship. He shone with such brilliant radiance that the entire vessel was illuminated as brightly as if it were day. And he said to the holy youth, "Greetings, Abanoub, beloved of God! And blessings to all who shall come to believe through you! Take strength and do not let your heart be discouraged. I shall bestow upon you all that you have asked and provide for you all the fortitude you shall need. I will give you words with which to answer the prince and will lead faithfully you until you receive the glorious reward of the imperishable crown of holy martyrdom!" And, having said this, be gave Abanoub a sign of peace and departed once more to the radiant vault of the Heavens.

After this, they continued their voyage to the south, until they came to a certain province known as Setpuphi. Three days later, they came to the district of Tuphot. They found there the governor of that place to be in the process of passing sentence upon Christians, pursuant to the edict of Diocletian. At that time, the governor had put to death a certain holy man, Paesi, together with his sister Thecla, and a very old priest as well. Each of these had been beheaded and their bodies cast amongst a thicket of thorn bushes. And none of the faithful were able to recover the bodies to give them an honorable burial, for fear of the troops who had been placed as guards around that place.

When the ship had arrived at the shore, the soldiers from the ship mingled freely with the local soldiers of Tuphot. They told each other about all the things that had transpired in their provinces and all they had witnessed. And thus they sat together and ate, drank and conversed for the whole day.

When the ninth hour of the day had arrived,[49] a certain woman boarded the ship. She had been blind and deaf since her birth and was also possessed by an unclean spirit. This unclean spirit cried out through the mouth of the woman, "You have lived well, you servant of Christ and scion of northern Egypt, O holy Abanoub! God has now summoned you to your final combat. You shall indeed pour out your blood nobly and heroically for the sake of the Name of Christ—just as your brother in the Faith, Paesi, has already done here, together with his sister Thecla, and a certain elderly priest. O Abanoub, destined martyr of God, I—who am a demon—have possessed this woman now for forty-six years. During this time, I have often plunged her into the waters and hurled her into fire. But now I have come before you, for your prayers to the omnipotent Deity have compelled me to do so. I know that you have the power to cast me out from this woman. But, St. Abanoub, I beg of you merely this—when you force me to leave this woman, that you permit me to take flight to the depths of the Red Sea and seek refuge there!"

But the saint replied to the demon, "I shall by no means permit you to flee, until you have first taken control of these wicked governors. You shall afflict them, and prevent them either from eating or drinking, until we have arrived at Alexandria." The demon gladly agreed to this.

Working through the body of the woman whom it inhabited, it seized from the governors' hands the goblets from which they were then drinking. It smashed them over their heads and spoke out, saying, "You fools, who refuse to worship the God of Heaven, and instead adore lifeless idols! Are you not ashamed to sit here, eating and drinking, whilst holy Abanoub is being detained within the hull of your ship?" The governors, who knew that the woman was mute, were astonished. They

---

49 That is, three o'clock in the afternoon.

were filled with dread at what had taken place, and were unable either to eat or to drink for the whole remainder of the voyage to Alexandria.

The governor of Tuphot said to the troops from Athribis, "My brothers, arise! Please continue with your journey, and take this magician away from my province. Do not permit anyone to see him here, lest they should be converted to this Faith of his!" So the soldiers and crew all made ready to sail from there once again. However, the woman, who had been possessed by the demon, now cried out in a loud voice, "My Lord Jesus Christ truly lives! I vow that I shall not leave this ship, but will continue with you on your voyage to the place where you are taking blessed Abanoub. There, like him, I also shall give up my life as a martyr for Christ!" The soldiers seized her and attempted to throw her off the ship onto the shore. But the woman clasped the railings of the ship firmly and cried out with a tremendous clamor. So one of the soldiers drew his sword and severed the woman's head with a single blow. And thus she, who had been vexed by a demon for many years, merited to be numbered amongst the glorious company of holy martyrs, receiving her crown of immortal beatitude on the twenty-seventh day of the month of Paoni.[50]

After this, the ship set forth with St. Abanoub, turning to the north, and arrived at the great city of Alexandria on second day of the month of Epip.[51] There they found the prince Armenius to have established his tribunal of judgement for the purpose of trying Christians, and to have executed already a great number of the faithful. The soldiers handed him the letter of the governors, in which the case of Abanoub was committed to his authority. He read it carefully, and was astonished at

---

50 July 4.
51 July 9.

the report of the fortitude which the youth had exhibited. He enquired as to where he currently was being detained, and the soldiers informed him that he remained in the hold of the ship. Armenius commanded that he should be brought before him at his tribunal of judgement without delay, with the soldiers keeping careful guard over him. When he was brought before the governor, Abanoub said, "O, this is my place of trial and of sentence! I have come here today, armed with the strength of my Lord Jesus Christ."

When Armenius beheld the youth he was struck by his handsome appearance and noble bearing. He said to him, "Lo! When I first saw you enter, I was filled with love for you, as if you were my very own son! But when I hear you mention the Name of Jesus, you become odious to me. My son, obey me and abandon this Name! For it shall not be useful or helpful to you at all. Indeed, many people have already forfeited their lives on account of this superstition. What does this Name of Jesus matter to you? He was crucified by the Jews, who hung Him from a cross while He claimed to be the Son of God. And He was not able to save even Himself, until they had put Him to death."

St. Abanoub, filled with pious indignation, replied to the prince;

> *"Close your mouth and be silent, you carnivorous beast! God shall destroy you with the breath of His mouth. Dogs and birds of carrion shall devour your wretched flesh! Your dwelling place for all eternity shall be the abyss of infernal blackness and fire, where the worm does not die[52] and where the gnashing of teeth never ceases.*

---

52 Isaiah 66:24. Mark 9:48.

As for me, I believe in my Lord Jesus Christ, the God who created both Heaven and earth.

I believe that He suffered for the sake of our sins.

I believe that He died and rose again from the dead, and that He now reigns supreme in incorruptible immortality.

I believe He lay in the silence of the tomb for three days.

I believe that he rose from the dead, and ascended into the glory of the Heavens, where He now sits at the right hand of God the Father.

And He shall truly come again to judge the living and the dead, to repay each according to their deeds.

You, you rabid cur, together with your godless emperor Diocletian and your foolish Apollo—you shall all be cast into the abyss of darkness, into the infernal depth of hell, for all eternity!"

Upon hearing this bold affirmation of Faith and fearsome condemnation of evil, Armenius boiled over with fury. He ordered Abanoub to be thrown on the ground on his back. He directed that ten sharp rods of iron be brought in and made red hot in the fire. Then these were used to pierce through the saint's body. Two were driven through his eyeballs, until they came out through his neck. Two were driven into his ears; two, through his chest; two, through each of his hands; and two, through his feet. Thus his entire body was severely mutilated, and seared with the burning heat of the iron. Next, he ordered ropes to be tied to his feet and him to be dragged down into the deepest dungeon. There the holy youth lay, brutally wounded and, indeed, half-dead.

But in the middle of the night, as he lay in the torments of unspeakable pain, he prayed with the sincerity of heartfelt tears, "My Lord Jesus Christ, you once heard the prayers of the three young men in the furnace, and made the flames become to them like mild dew![53] You heard the prayers of the prophet Daniel from the lion's pit, and You sustained him therein with Divine nourishment, so that He glorified You, O God.[54] You freed the righteous woman, Susanna, from the hands of the prevaricators and slanderers who attempted to destroy her.[55] O Lord, liberate me also today from the grasp of these godless tyrants!"

And while these words were still upon his lips, the archangel Suriel appeared, and stood in the middle of his prison cell. He said to the saint, "Be brave, O Abanoub, blessed martyr of my Lord Jesus Christ, and take comfort. I am Suriel, the archangel of God! The Lord has sent me to you to give you fortitude and strength in all the tortures which have been inflicted upon you, and in all the afflictions and sufferings which you are destined to undergo." And he passed his hands over the injured body of the blessed youth, removing the iron spikes that had been driven into him. And as he did so, Abanoub's wounds were miraculously healed and he was infused with marvelous strength and vitality. Then, whilst the saint looked on, the archangel ascended once more into the Heavens surrounded by glory.

---

53 Cf. Daniel 3.
54 Cf. Daniel 14:29-40.
55 Cf. Susanna (Daniel 13).

VI

When the light of morning arose, the prince ordered his tribunal to be set up in the center of the city of Alexandria. He directed the idols representing the gods Apollo, Jupiter, Athena, Artemis and all the other Roman deities to be brought in and placed upon thrones. And when the prince himself, Artemis, arrived, he commanded Abanoub to be brought before him, [if he was still alive]. But when the guards arrived at the prison, they were surprised to find Abanoub—not only still alive—but exultant and joyful and blessing God. When they led him before the prince, they said, "Here he is, the one who has been disturbing the crowds so much! We bring him before your Highness, so that you may do to him what you like."

As he took his place before the tribunal, the prince demanded of him that, [for the purposes of judgement,] he declare his name and his province of origin.[56] But Abanoub said to him, "Listen to me, you wicked prince! Why should you ask me my name? Or my province of origin? What concern are such things

---

56 There is a slight narrative inconsistency apparent here, as Armenius must surely have already been aware of who Abanoub was and whence he came when he ordered him to be brought into his presence. Nevertheless, it is possible that stating his name and home province was a necessary formal part of the legal proceedings. Presumably it was for this reason, rather than any actual uncertainty as to his identity, that Armenius asks him for these now.

to you?" But Armenius responded, "Are you not afraid to speak to *me* with such impertinence? Do you not know that I am the prince and ruler of this city, and that you are entirely under my power?" Abanoub answered, "It is written in the holy Gospel according to St. Matthew: 'Fear not those who can destroy the body, but are not able to kill the soul. Fear rather the one who is able to destroy both body and soul in the fire of hell.'[57] Do to me whatever you please! You may have power over my body, but my soul belongs entirely to Christ. You wicked and foolish scoundrel! Indeed, I *wish* to undergo all the punishments you can inflict, so that I may be made worthy of eternal life in the Kingdom of Heaven. The torments you can inflict are but passing and momentary—they are nothing! But the peace and joy which my Lord Jesus Christ offers are eternal. Do to me as you please, for I shall never give worship to your idols!"

The prince snapped back, "I perceive that you pour out many words before me! Yet still, you have not given your name and your home province. State these clearly, I command you!" The saint said to him, "Abanoub is my name. I am from the town of Nehisa in the province of Nimesoti."

The prince continued, "Well, Abanoub, listen to me now, and I shall say one thing to you. Life and death are placed before you; choose which of these you will! Do you not see the [splendid] beauty of this idol of Apollo? There is, indeed, none to compare with him in the whole world. Follow my instructions, and offer due sacrifice to the gods. If you do this, I shall bestow upon you many honors and favors." But the noble youth replied with resolution, "You impious and filthy wretch! Since the time I left my native province until I have arrived here, I have been subject to many and varied tortures. But no one has been able to deceive me into making sacrifice to these abominable idols.

---

57 Matthew 10:28.

Why should I now obey you and offer sacrifice to your mindless Apollo, and abandon my true Lord, Jesus Christ? He shall certainly destroy you, together with your father, Satan,[58] and your godless superiors and emperor!"

Upon this, the prince was infuriated. He ordered Abanoub to be subjected to further tortures. But his soldiers said to him, "Your Highness, our Prince! Already we have tortured this prisoner very much, yet he remains completely unaffected and unmoved. But there are three men here at the moment, who are snake charmers and have many serpents in their possession. We suggest that these serpents be released upon the prisoner, so that they may consume his flesh and bones altogether!" The prince, very pleased by this proposal, ordered the three snake charmers to be brought to him. And, accordingly, they came before him.

Armenius said to them, "Bring to me some snakes which are full of venom and fury, so that they may kill and consume this equally toxic youth! If you are able to succeed in this thing I shall reward you very generously for your services." The snake charmers then departed, and returned with some ten specially chosen, extremely deadly serpents. They said to the prince, "Your Highness, may you live forever! If you had here two hundred men, or even three hundred men, these snakes would destroy them all within a single hour."

Upon hearing this Armenius exulted with malicious joy. He commanded that Abanoub be thrown into his darkest dungeon and the serpents be released upon him. Now one of these serpents was of some thirty feet in length. And they were all ferocious creatures and of terrifying appearance. When he saw them, Armenius was delighted, and was confident that they would soon kill and devour Abanoub. He said to himself,

---

58 Cf. John 8:44.

"By the great god Apollo! These shall certainly overcome this troublesome rebel!"

But as soon as the snakes beheld holy Abanoub and sensed his sanctity and innocence, they pressed themselves to the ground in veneration of him! And the archangel Michael stood by young Abanoub and made all the serpents become gentle and tame towards him. And the cell, which had hitherto been enveloped in pitch darkness, now radiated with light as if illuminated by the midday sun. Then Michael imparted to the saint something of his own celestial fortitude and courage, and then ascended once more into the Heavens in splendid glory.

When dawn arrived, the prince eagerly called to himself the prison guards and instructed them to see whether the serpents had killed and devoured Abanoub. But when they opened the door of the cell, they found the saint to be there peacefully praying, while the snakes were before him, in peaceful veneration. They led him to the governor, and the snakes faithfully followed behind him in his footsteps, as if they were his pets! The whole crowd who witnessed this wondrous thing were utterly amazed. They gave glory to God and honor to Abanoub, proclaiming, "There is one God only, and that is the God in whom St. Abanoub has place his Faith! Truly, there is no deity except for Him!"

Armenius was enraged, and exclaimed, "Verily, there has never been a magician similar to this one!" But Abanoub retorted, "How wrong you are to say that the servants of God are magicians! But now you shall see a real miracle worked!" At this, he said to one of the snakes, "Hear me, O serpent! I command you in the name of my Lord Jesus Christ that you go forth and become as a noose around the neck of this impious fiend!" Immediately the reptile sprang up, and wound itself firmly around the neck of Armenius. He cried out in panic, saying, "Abanoub, I adjure you through your Lord Jesus Christ! Have mercy upon me, and spare my life."

And all the officials who were present stood up and beseeched Abanoub to free their leader from the attack of the deadly serpent. So the blessed youth spoke again to the snake and commanded him, in the name of the Lord Jesus Christ, to release itself from the neck of Armenius. Immediately the serpent did so and fell to the ground. The whole crowd looked on in wonder and astonishment. Even the three snake charmers were amazed. They declared, "We now believe in the Lord Jesus Christ, the God whose power has permitted Abanoub to do this stupendous thing!" And many of those present also proclaimed themselves to be converted to the Christian Faith.

[But Armenius, though relieved to be rescued from the snake, remained stubbornly unmoved in his heart. He therefore ordered the execution of all those who now confessed themselves to be Christian. And thus all those who had been converted,] who numbered some thirty-five souls, were beheaded at the edge of the sword, on the eighth day of the month of Epip.[59]

After this Armenius said to the saint, "O Abanoub, by the great god Apollo! Unless you obey me and cease from these works of trickery, I shall put you to a most dreadful death without mercy!" But Abanoub exclaimed, "You fool! To the wise man a single word of instruction is sufficient, but a fool will never be taught. Are you not ashamed, you wicked wretch, to tell me to deny my God when you yourself have seen and experienced His power and mercy?"

The wicked and proud prince was consumed with wrath. He ordered an iron cauldron to be brought in, and it to be filled with sulphur, pitch, oil, lead and bitumen. Then he had a fire lit

---

59 July 15.

underneath it, until the flames reach ten feet into the air and the ghastly mixture boiled furiously. Then he had his guards throw St. Abanoub into the cauldron!

The whole crowd of onlookers were greatly alarmed and horrified and cried out in distress. Yet all the Christians present strove to offer him words of comfort and encouragement, including a certain Julius of Aqfahs. And they witnessed the tremendous endurance and fortitude of the blessed youth in the face of such horrendous torture. [The prince and his officials, along with most of the crowd, then departed. Julius remained, though, to witness the outcome of the dreadful proceedings.][60]

St. Abanoub, from the midst of the boiling mixture, raised his hands in prayer, saying;

> *"Give ear to my cry, my Lord Jesus Christ! Truly, I am your servant, and the son of your handmaid.*[61] *Hear my voice from the middle of the flames! You see, O Lord, the waves of the boiling liquid rise above my head. Lord Jesus Christ, look mercifully upon my misery and my exile.*
>
> *If it is your will that I should complete my battle in the middle of this fire, take now my spirit from me*

---

60 This is not in the original text, but added by the translator to clarify the narrative sense. Since a little later Abanoub will sit down with Julius while he commits the story of all that he has undergone to writing (which must have been a fairly lengthy process), it seems clear that the crowd was no longer present at that time. Moreover, Armenius will later send soldiers to see whether or not Abanoub has been consumed by the flames, so presumably he must have departed also. It seems to be consistent with these elements of the narrative for Armenius and the crowd to have departed at some point prior to Abanoub's prayer and the appearance of Christ to him, and hence this small insertion is proposed here.

61 Psalm 116:16.

quickly! Otherwise, O Lord, send forth Your angel
that he may strengthen and protect me. For Yours
is the glory for all eternity. Amen."

And behold! At this point the Savior Himself descended from Heaven in a chariot of refulgent glory. He was accompanied by the archangels Michael and Gabriel, at His right and at His left respectively, as well as an innumerable multitude of seraphim and cherubim. And immediately the flames subsided and were extinguished. Indeed, they became to St. Abanoub like a gentle breeze suffused with cool dew. And Michael gently lifted up the saint out of the cauldron and placed him on the ground. There he stood, perfectly well and without the slightest trace of injury or harm.

The Savior then spoke to him thus:

"Be strong, my brave warrior, Abanoub, and take
comfort! For I, Jesus your King, am with you.
The time of your victory draws nigh, my beloved
Abanoub. I have arisen and come to you, so that
I may show to you the wonderful crown of light
which shall be yours.

Behold, I have prepared three splendid crowns
which I shall place upon your head. The first of
these is for your departure and exile from your
native land. The second is a reward for the blood
you have shed for the Faith. And the third is for
all the pains and tortures you have endured for the
sake of My Name.

My chosen one, I have made ready for you one who shall treat your body with reverence and return it to your native province to bury it honorably there.

And for whosoever shall write down the story of your heroic sufferings and martyrdom, I shall instruct Enoch, the scribe of Divine justice,[62] to erase the sentence due for their sins and to write their name in the Book of Life. I myself shall bless them in all that they do upon the earth.

Whoever vows to make an offering or to give alms upon your tomb, I shall bless upon the earth and shall repay them sevenfold.

Whoever shall be called by your name in the Faith, I shall bless, together with all his household, and shall liberate him from all evils.

To all pregnant mothers who are struggling to give birth, and reverently call to mind your holy name in prayer—I shall grant to them their offspring alive and healthy.

And as for the province where your body shall rest and which shall venerate you in my name—I shall generously bless that entire province.

And I shall place my servant, the archangel Suriel, as a guardian for your tomb, to keep watch over it until the end of the world!"

---

62 Enoch is identified as the scribe responsible for keeping records in Heaven in the non-canonical Book of Enoch (Cf. Enoch 12:3-4).

Once He had said all these things to St. Abanoub, the Savior then ascended to the Heavens in His glory.

VII

Now as the Savior had been speaking to Abanoub, He had caused the eyes of Julius, [who had remained present,] to be opened. Thus, Julius was able to perceive the Savior speaking to the saint. He therefore arose and approached the holy youth. He prostrated himself in veneration before him, saying, "Blessed are you, O happy youth! For you have confounded both rulers and governors. Blessed are you and blessed is the womb that carried you! Blessed in the province is which you were born! And blessed shall be the person who preserves and honors your memory upon the earth, O holy martyr of Christ, St. Abanoub! I implore you, through all the tortures and pains which you have so courageously endured, and for the Name of Christ, that you sit and take your rest here with me for a while, so that I may write down all the things which my eyes have seen and which my ears have heard concerning you."

The blessed Abanoub said to Julius, "My dear father, I ask of you that you kindly bring me a little water to drink." This he did, and the youth drank forthwith. Then he said, "May my Lord Jesus Christ give to you the water of life! May He forgive your sins. O man of God, Julius of Aqfahs, you shall never experience punishment, for all eternity! I beseech of you a favor, my dear

Julius; please fulfill this request of my soul. Stay with me until I have consummated my battle for the Faith and completed my martyrdom. After this, gather my body and deliver it to the land of my ancestors. May it rest there until it should please my Lord Jesus Christ to reveal its location. I am an inhabitant of northern Egypt, in the province of Nimesoti, in the tiny village of Nehisa, which is a little to the south of the river."

Julius then took a blank codex, and wrote in it the narrative of all the tortures and sufferings which St. Abanoub had undergone. And he said to him, "My dear brother in Christ, I am ready to do all that you have asked of me." After this they both arose and prayed. And the saint bestowed his blessing upon Julius the scribe, who then departed, leaving the holy youth next to the cauldron.

After this the prince Armenius said to his soldiers, who had earlier set up the boiling cauldron to kill St. Abanoub, "Go to the place where you set up the cauldron and see whether this great wizard and deceiver is still alive or whether he has been cooked in the fire!" This they did, and to their surprise discovered Abanoub peacefully sitting next to the cauldron, drinking cool water from a jug—just like someone who is taking pleasant relief from a hot summer's day! He was blessing God, saying, "I give you thanks, my Lord Jesus Christ, for You have heard my prayer and freed me from my affliction. You have led me forth from the depths of the inferno and have given rest to my heart when I was beset with anguish. I bless You, my Lord Jesus Christ, who have made me rejoice in my salvation! Yours is the glory, together with Your Heavenly Father and the Holy Spirit, for all eternity. Amen."

Before he had completed the "Amen" in this prayer, the guards seized him and dragged him before the tribunal of judgement. They announced to Armenius, "Your Highness, look, we have found the prisoner Abanoub sitting by the cauldron, sipping cool water from a jug and blessing his God, Jesus Christ!" When Armenius saw the saint standing before him, perfectly well, he was filled with Satanic envy. He cried out, "I am plunged into worries by this type of Christian, and in particular by this wretched youth! Quite rightly Cyprian, the governor of Athribis, wrote that he was unable to gain victory against this master magician." And he was stupefied and bewildered for a long period of time.

When Julius saw that Armenius was perplexed, he approach him and said, "O prince Armenius, if you will take my advice, you should carry out the sentence of death against this youth promptly and in a straightforward manner, and then you will have some rest. But if you try to afflict worse tortures upon him, his God shall certainly rescue him from your clutches and you shall be confounded before all the people. Therefore, I urge you, carry out your sentence of death upon him without delay, in order that you may have some rest!" Julius, in fact, said this [because he knew that Abanoub was destined by God to be martyred,] and in order that the blessed youth would be spared from further cruel tortures. Indeed, he always took the greatest care for all the saints and welcomed their blessings sincerely.

Armenius agreed with this suggestion, since he realized that he was not going to be able to prevail against the fortitude and endurance of Abanoub by means of any tortures, however dreadful. So, he ordered that he be put to death immediately, saying, "Abanoub of Nehisa is a member of the sect of the Christians. He does not obey the orders of me, the legitimate ruler of this place. Nor does he pay the required worship to the gods. Therefore I sentence him to be led forth from the city, and there for his head to be removed by the sword. Let it be done!" So some executioners, armed with spears, seized Abanoub by both his arms and dragged him out of the city, going a little to the south of it. They took him to a high, rocky place, where they were to behead him.

When the blessed youth had arrived at the place where he was to complete his battle for the Faith, he said to the executioners, "My brothers, I implore you, have patience with me! Permit me to pray to my God for a short time, that He will accept from me my soul." They granted him the requested permission, and accordingly he prayed;

> *"My Lord Jesus Christ, for the sake of all the torments I have undergone, receive now my soul in this blessed hour! You know, O Lord, that it is for the sake of this hour that I have passed through so many sufferings.*
>
> *Let the torments of hell flee from me and all the dreadful faces of grim horror! Let the river of infernal fire become calm in my presence until I shall have crossed over it. May all the evil powers, which exist to punish sinners, flee from my presence. May your angels of light accept my soul, to bear it hence into the realm of celestial glory.*
>
> *Lord, grant grace to my body—so that all who are afflicted by illness or weakness or tormented by fever or by chill, or by any infirmity whatsoever, may, if they come to my tomb to pray to Your holy Name, be healed by You. For Yours is the glory forever and ever. Amen."*

Once he had completed his prayer, two soldiers took hold of his arms. An executioner then raised his sword, and with a single blow cleanly took off the saint's head. Immediately there flowed forth blood and pure milk. And thus Abanoub gave forth his spirit on the twenty-fourth day of the month of Epip,[63] a Sunday, at the ninth hour of the day.[64]

Julius of Aqfahs waited until the middle of the night, and then went forth to the place of execution and collected the body of the saint. He wrapped him in a burial sheet and anointed his body with perfumes, oil and wine. He then had him placed upon a ship with three of his servants. These sailed firstly to the south for three days, to a province by the name of Sethnuphi. Next they sailed northwards, against the river, and sought there the province of Nimesoti.

When some men from Abanoub's village heard about this, they rejoice greatly. They went out and met the servants of Julius and led them, together with the body of St. Abanoub, to the village of Nehisa. There, they buried his body in secret in a small tomb, and kept it concealed until the persecution of the Christians [under Diocletian] had come to an end. After this, the villages built a church at the site of his tomb, as a fitting token of veneration. All those who had been martyred [during this wave of persecution,] along with St. Abanoub, numbered some 19,086 souls; each of whom accepted an immortal crown of glory in the Kingdom of Heaven.

I have narrated to you now all the things which happened to St. Abanoub, the brave martyr of Christ. I, who testify to these events, am the same Julian of Aqfahs mentioned in these writings. The holy youth, St. Abanoub, consummated the glorious battle of his martyrdom on the twenty-fourth day of the month of Epip.[65] He thus received an imperishable crown of victory in the Kingdom of our Lord Jesus Christ—to whom be

---

63 July 31.
64 That is, three o'clock in the afternoon.
65 July 31.

all glory, honor and adoration, together with the Father and the life-giving Spirit, now and always and for ages unending. Amen.

The Martyrdom of
St. Apatil of Sabaru

The Martyrdom of St. Apatil, the Martyr of Christ, who nobly consummated his battle [for the Faith] on the sixteenth day of the month of Epip,[66] in the Peace of God. Amen.

I

It happened, during the reign of the godless emperor Diocletian, in the third year of his reign, that he initiated a great persecution against all Christians,[67] carried out throughout the entire world. Many struggled bravely for the name of Christ. They proclaimed with great courage and unwavering fidelity His glorious Resurrection from the dead, His ascension into Heaven, and His assuming of His seat at the right hand of the Father. And these all, as martyrs, obtained the crown due to their heroic profession of the faith from our Lord and Savior, Jesus Christ.

Now, this godless fiend—I mean the wicked emperor Diocletian—wrote an edict to all places under his command, which read thus:

> *I, the Emperor Diocletian Caesar, extend greetings to all the peoples and races who are under my command, and who live by the providence of the gods.*

---

66 July 23.

67 The third year of Diocletian's reign would have been about 287 AD; but the commencement of the Diocletian persecution is normally given as about 303 AD. However, Diocletian's status as emperor varied greatly over the course of its history and went through various stages (at various point there were rival claimants to the throne and co-emperors), so the year meant by the "third year of his reign" is not absolutely clear. It seems probable that the year meant here would coincide with the commencement of the time which is customarily referred to as the "Diocletian persecution" (i.e. 303 AD).

It has come to my attention that [the sect of] the Christians worship one God only, Jesus Christ. They treat with scorn all other gods, especially Apollo, who is the protector of the whole world—and who has granted to me all my triumphs. Therefore, I have issued to these Christians a commandment that they dispense with their inane pretension, and offer proper worship to all the gods, who preserve this world and grant to kings their victories. And regarding whomsoever does not obey this, our glorious decree, promulgated by the noble senate— they are to be subjected to all forms of punishment and tortures, without mercy. This I command to all leaders, governors and magistrates in every province from great Rome to Egypt, including Pentapolis and Africa, Great Marés; and, indeed, from Libya to Ethiopia.

If these Christians renounce their error, they are to be spared. But if they persist in their Faith, our authority hereby commands that, after they have been subject to every form of torture, they be put to death by the sword and their bodies be incinerated. We issue this decree with the greatest reverence for the gods, through whom we have all received so many benefits, and by whose immortal providence we live! May our will in this matter come to fruition.

This edict was sent to Egypt, where it was delivered to Armenius, the prince of Alexandria, by a certain imperial emissary by the name of Dionysius. Armenius received him with a kiss of honor. He then summoned to himself Arius, the governor, and Ammon, the director of works, together with a great multitude of troops, and had them assemble in the city of Alexandria. When they were assembled together, he ordered the edict to be read aloud to them all.

The contents of the edict having been heard, many soldiers, led by Arius the governor, went forth throughout the whole of the region of Egypt, from Alexandria to Great Marés and as far south as Ethiopia. They seized innumerable Christians. Some were slaughtered by the sword, and their flesh thrown to dogs, beasts or birds of prey. Others were burnt with fire. But in the midst of all this [violence and cruelty], God glorified His chosen ones. For countless miracles and wonders were performed through these martyrs. [By means of these miracles,] the worshippers of Christ were given consolation [and encouragement], while the godless were confounded and their wickedness revealed. [Thus those responsible for the persecution] were shown to be destined for condemnation at the Day of Judgement to be brought about by God, when punishment shall be given to all impious apostate souls who have deserted Him.

While all of these things were taking place, a not inconsiderable degree of consternation and a great fear arose amongst all Christian souls. Now there was a certain holy and God-fearing priest by the name of Sotericus. He lived in the province of Sabaru, in the tiny village of Timui Psati, which was near one of the great cities of Egypt. He was a just man and well advanced in age. He had two sons; one called Apatil and the other called John. Both were righteous and diligent worshippers of God. St. Apatil was a handsome youth and filled with Faith and the Holy Spirit. When he was sixteen years old, he was, against the will of his father, conscripted into the army. He was assigned to the military barracks known as Babylon, which was to the south of the city of Ombos,[68] and had as its tribune a man called Callinicus. While stationed there, St. Apatil devoted himself to holy exercises and ascetic labors. He offered many prayers, day and night, accompanied by an abundance of tears of compunction and piety. Furthermore, he performed works of mercy and gave generously to the poor and orphans, as much as he possibly could.

When the governor Arius first arrived at the barracks of Babylon, Apatil happened to be alone in a certain secret place, where he would go in private to pray zealously to God, with many fervent tears. He would pray especially that God would bring to an end the persecution of Christians which was then afflicting His flock, save them from the trials and tribulations they confronted, and restore His Church to peace. When he had completed his prayers according to his custom, he rested for a while, and fell asleep. Then the Lord appeared to him in a vision, in the form of a very handsome and radiant young man. He said to Apatil, "Why do you sleep, when there is a battle going on?! Arise and fight for my Name, and you shall be rewarded with a crown! Once you have courageously completed your noble battle by profession of the Faith, I shall lead you to my Father and offer you to Him as a gift. In this your joy will exceed all words! Therefore have no fear of any tortures, for I shall be with you throughout all your afflictions which you shall undergo for the sake of my name. Be a strong athlete [of the Faith]!"

When the good Savior had said these things to him, Apatil beheld Him no more. At that time dawn was rising. The governor had his tribunal of judgement set up in the barracks and commanded all to assemble before him. When they had all gathered he read to them the edict of the emperor, and instructed them to give

---

68 Modern day Naqaba.

due worship to the [Roman] gods. As if with one heart and mind, the officers and soldiers all prostrated themselves, and adored the pagan idols. But St. Apatil, who was in the middle of them, remained standing alone, refusing to make any adoration, nor even bowing his head.

The governor saw him standing there and commanded that he be led to him immediately. He demanded of him, "Why do you not worship the gods, in accordance with the imperial decree?" The saint replied, "I worship the God of Heaven, who is my true King! He is the Savior of all creation, both visible and invisible, and in His hands is the breath of every living being. He it is who establishes and deposes kings, and who casts fear and awe into the hearts of potentates. He nourishes all creation, for the sake of His own great love for humankind." Upon hearing this, the governor was inflamed with wrath and said to Apatil, "You fool! I shall indeed punish you for this impudent speech you have made."

The governor then had Apatil wrapped with chains and ordered four soldiers to drag him around, causing him to fall violently many times. But the saint cried out to the Lord, saying, "My Lord Jesus Christ, help me for in You alone have I placed all my hopes!" And when he had said this, behold, an angel of the Lord touched him and gave him comfort. And immediately the chains became unbound! He stood calmly in front of the governor, without any pain or injury apparent on his body whatsoever. The governor ground his teeth in fury, filled with a desire to kill him. And on that same day, this wicked wretch, Arius, passed sentence of death upon believers, who received in return a crown of victory from Christ, their true beloved.

Regarding Apatil, he ordered his ankles to be pierced and ropes to be threaded through them. Then he commanded him to be dragged over a place covered with sharp gravel until his blood gushed forth over the earth. After this, he had his soldiers set up and light an immense bonfire in the middle of the military compound. When the flames burned intensely, he ordered the blessed man to be bound and cast into the midst of the blaze. But truly God, who looks upon the struggles of the just, is always prompt to hear the supplications and pleas of those who place their hopes in Him. Accordingly, He looked with gracious mercy upon the battle which St. Apatil was then undergoing for the sake of His own holy Name. He made dense clouds appear all around him, which began at once to pour forth heavy rain! And the fire was immediately extinguished.

And, behold, the voice of the Lord thundered from Heaven, "Be strong and take courage! I am with you, and truly I shall liberate you! Never shall I abandon you in your need." When Apatil heard this voice he was filled with the strength of the Lord and all the pains and injuries which his body bore instantly disappeared from him. And he was placed, standing before the governor, without any sign of harm or distress. The crowds of onlookers, when they perceived this wondrous thing, exclaimed, "Great is the God of the Christians! Verily, the God in whom Apatil believes is the only God!" The governor, when he heard this uproar of the crowd, [was perplexed about what course of action he should take.] So he ordered Apatil to be held in custody until he could receive advice on the matter. The saint was therefore led away to prison.

While he was being detained there he performed many miracles and wonders, as if he were himself one of the elect apostles of Christ. Indeed, he healed the sick, cast out demons, cured people of all manner of affliction, by the power of our Lord Jesus Christ which abided in him.

But when the fame which his miracles and healing generated came to the attention of the governor, he was extremely angry.

He said to his nobles who were around him, "What should be do with this magician, Apatil? Indeed, he is drawing all people to believe in the Faith he holds and to support him, because of these works of wizardry he is performing." His nobles replied thus, "Our lord the Governor, let us not torture him here, for a great multitude support him. Indeed, they are all deceived by the magical arts which he possesses. Rather, let our lord the Governor send him to the city of Peremun, to Pompius the governor of that city. He can be tortured there. But let us not proceed with his torture in this place, lest we be obliged to execute also the entire crowd of his supporters!"

And so Arius the governor wrote an epistle to Pompius, the governor of Peremun. His missive read as follows:

> *Arius, the Governor of Thebaid, to Pompius, the Governor of Peremun: Greetings! Following the commands of the Emperor, it behooves us to perform all due service and ministries due to the imperial throne and to the glorious and immortal gods, in order that we may live by their providence and receive honor from the same. Therefore, in accordance with the edict of our emperor Diocletian, I send to you Apatil, a soldier of the barracks of Babylon, who has been found to be a criminal. For when we found him to be defying the mandates of our Emperor—the lover of humanity—and of the glorious senate, and to be deceived by the error of the Christians and worshipping the one whom they call Christ, we questioned him very thoroughly [and found him to be guilty]. We now entrust him to your power and judgement, that you may hear*

him publicly, and impose a sentence upon him in accordance with the imperial laws. We wish you well, in all honor of the glorious gods!

And so Apatil, bound in chains, was led to Peremun, and made to stand before Pompius the governor and the troops who attended him. And his attendants presented to Pompius the letter of Arius. When he had duly read this document, he commanded that Apatil should be placed into prison until the following day, for it was then already evening.

II

When the next day arrived, Pompius, the governor of Peremun, ordered the saint to be brought before him. Immediately his officials led him in, secured with chains. And the governor questioned him, "Are you Apatil, the magician, who the most excellent Arianus, the governor of Thebaid, has sent to us?" The saint answered, saying, "Certainly, I am Apatil. But I am no magician. God forbid that I should be one! However, I am a Christian and a servant of Christ, the true God."

The governor then said to Apatil, "If you wish to be saved, abandon this error of yours! Rather, worship the truth and acknowledge the immortal gods who preserve the entire world in its existence. In this way, you shall be as a son to us, and we shall indeed delight in your loyal service." But the blessed martyr of Christ responded thus, "O you prince of evil, and advocate of the powers of darkness! You are a friend of perdition, a son of the devil and an enemy of all truth.[69] Are you not ashamed to try to persuade a servant of Christ to apostasy, merely so that he can evade the persecutions of the godless, the wicked and prevaricators—that is to say, people like you? You may

---

69 Cf. Acts 13:10.

hear me. I hereby declare openly that I am a Christian and I worship the God of the Christians. I despise the emperor and his abominable gods, with whom you shall be thrown into the hell of eternal fire, together with the demons whom you adore! For it is indeed written, 'There the worm shall not die, nor the fires be extinguished.'[70]"

The governor, hearing this, raged furiously like a wild beast. He commanded that the fingernails and toenails be ripped from the saint's hands and feet, and his eyeballs to be pulled out. Afterwards, he had a mixture of vinegar and ash poured into his open wounds. As St. Apatil endured these cruel tortures, he prayed, saying;

> *"My Lord Jesus Christ, Savior of all creation, you rescue all those who have Faith in You. You are a safe harbor for all those who are afflicted, and salvation for all who are oppressed. Come to me now, O Lord! Help me, and save me in the great need in which I find myself at this present time, lest the pagans should say 'Where is his God?'[71] For You are the God to whom all glory is due, together with Your Heavenly Father and the life-giving Holy Spirit, both now and forever! Amen."*

As soon as Apatil pronounced the "Amen" at the conclusion of this prayer, the angel of the Lord touched him and healed him. All his limbs and members, as well as his eyes, were restored to their previous condition, without the slightest trace of injury or harm. The governor was astonished, and exclaimed, "How great are the magical powers of these Christians!" And the

---

70 Isaiah 66:24. Mark 9:48.

71 Cf. Psalm 42:10, Psalm 115:2.

surrounding multitude of onlookers all cried out, "There is no other God than the God of the Christians, Jesus Christ, the God of St. Apatil!"

Then the governor, [wishing to conciliate the crowd,] said to the blessed martyr of Christ, "If you simply follow my instructions, O Apatil, and offer the due sacrifice to the [official] gods, then I shall let you go freely, and you shall spare yourself from many and great torments." But Apatil replied, "It is written, 'Even if an army surrounds me, my heart will not fear. If war breaks out against me, in You, [O God,] shall I hope!'[72] Therefore I shall not fear your tortures and your threats will never be able to separate me from the love of my Lord Jesus Christ." The governor snapped back at him, "I shall teach [you to be rid of] your arrogance, you fool! And then you shall acknowledge the gods who preserve us." And he commanded him to be suspended from a stake and flayed, until his intestines were revealed.

As this was being done and his flesh and blood fell freely from his body, the saint was in immense pain. His vitality began to fade from him as his life started to fail him. But he cried out earnestly, saying, "Arise, O Lord, and help me! For on Your account, 'they kill us all day long, and we are counted as sheep for the slaughter.'[73] Arise, help me and free me for the sake of Your most holy Name, because in You alone I have placed my hopes!" And God, who once declared, "I shall say, 'Here I am!' to the one who prayed to me,"[74] now graciously deigned to hear His servant. Immediately an angel of the Lord came to Apatil and healed him. The chains which bound him were loosened, and there he stood before the governor, showing not the slightest trace of harm or injury.

---

72 Psalm 27:3.
73 Psalm 44:22.
74 Isaiah 58:9.

When the crowd saw this, they glorified God, exclaiming, "There is indeed no God but the God of the Christians! A curse be upon Diocletian and all his idols!" The governor was enraged at the sentiments of the crowd. He said to the saint, "I shall have you tortured upon the iron bed.[75] And then we shall see if your Jesus is able to free you from my hands!" To this, the saint responded, "He has liberated me already, and still He shall liberate me again! You should know that all your threats and torments have no power whatsoever to make me afraid. The flames with which you now threaten me are only passing; but they shall serve to recall the eternal flames in which shall burn your father, the devil,[76] and all the godless, who—like yourself—refuse to acknowledge the true God."

When he heard this, the governor ground his teeth in anger. He ordered the iron bed to be brought in and the saint to be secured upon it. Then he had a fire lit underneath it, and oil and fat cast upon the blaze, so that the flames leapt up ferociously, ready to incinerate the flesh of the holy man. Meanwhile, four groups of four soldiers stood around him and rained down hard blows upon him with rods. Yet in all of these things, God protected his faithful servant, not permitting him to succumb to these pains and torments.

The blessed martyr of Christ, St. Apatil, while the fire was still consuming him and he was being struck with inhuman cruelty, prayed to God thus;

> *"O God, You are enthroned above the cherubim,*
> *who proclaim the glory of Your Divinity in ceaseless*
> *and wondrous song!*

---

75 A device upon which prisoners were secured in order to be tortured.
76 Cf. John 9:44.

*You have been my firmament since I was in the
womb. You alone are my hope, whereby I drew
milk from my mother's breast.*

*Do not abandon me or desert me now, God my
Savior! For you are my protector, and the unfailing
help of all those who suffer on account of Your great
name.*

*Yours is the glory, together with the Heavenly Father
who begot You, and the Holy Spirit who gives life
to all, now and forever, and for all eternity! Amen."*

When he had concluded this prayer, by the power of God he
was suddenly lifted up and placed standing before the governor.
And there was no wound or injury or sign of harm upon his
body whatsoever. The assembled crowd, seeing this happen,
cried out in amazement and wonder, "Blessed is the God who
has liberated His servant Apatil from the flames! The God of the
Christians is truly the one God, and there is none other besides
Him!"

At this, the governor burned with uncontrollable rage and
stamped the ground with his feet in the manner of a wild beast.
He said, "Behold, Apatil! I will burn you in a fiercer fire than
this! And then I shall see whether or not your God is able to
free you from my hands!" This time, he commanded him to
be thrown into an enclosed furnace and locked in. He had the
fire ignited so that it burned with the greatest possible intensity.
And there he left the saint to remain for three days and three
nights.

But God looked down upon the great love and fidelity of his
servant Apatil. He did not permit him to perish, nor the godless
and wicked to glory in victory over the saint. Indeed, He sent

forth His angel, who quelled the flames of the blaze. The middle of the furnace, in which Apatil sat, was made cool and pleasant, as if a gentle breeze and mild dewfall were there. And neither harm nor pain came unto the body or soul of the righteous man.

Now St. Apatil, perceiving the assistance and protection which had come to him from the Lord, praised God, like the three young men [from the book of Daniel]. He sang,

> *"Blessed are You, Lord God of our fathers, and greatly blessed! Your name is full of glory forever and ever.[77] Amen.*
>
> *For you have indeed sent your angel, and liberated your servant from the torments of the fire. Nor have you permitted my enemies to triumph over me. Therefore, I shall proclaim Your name in the assemblies, and in the midst of the multitude shall I bless Your glory.*
>
> *Because of what You have done, O Lord, I shall rejoice unceasingly in Your salvation! Under Your wings shall I exult, for Yours is the glory forever and ever. Amen."*

And immediately, by the power of the omnipotent God, the saint was raised from the furnace, and placed before the governor. [He stood before him completely unharmed]. When he beheld this, the governor was utterly astonished, together with all those who were with him. He exclaimed, "By the gods! I am amazed that you are still alive!" The saint replied, "I did not tell you this was going to happen before [although I knew that it

---

77 Daniel 3:26.

would], in order that you yourself might witness the constancy and courage of the servants of the true God! Truly, it is always the will of our God to save those who sincerely believe in Him."

[But the governor still persisted in his incredulity,] and said "Never shall I believe your words! Will you offer sacrifice, or will you not?" The saint answered with undaunted courage, "Never shall I offer sacrifice! Do to me whatever you like."

Then the governor ordered him to be placed on a ship and taken out to sea, and, bound in heavy chains, to be thrown into the depths of the waters. But once the saint had been thrown into the sea he was, once again, drawn free by the power of God. And, as before, he was placed before the governor, before even the ship which had taken him out had returned. At this the governor grew agitated and was stupefied. He commanded that the saint be immediately sent back to prison, while he considered what he should do to him next.

III

Now there was a certain blind man who was held in the same prison. This blind man had completely lost his spirits [on account of his affliction.] St. Apatil, when he saw him, placed his hands over the blind man's eyes and made the sign of the cross, in the name of the Father, the Son and the Holy Spirit. He then breathed upon his face three times. At this, the man's sight was restored to him and he cried out in a loud voice, "There is no other God except for You, O Lord Jesus Christ, the God of the blessed martyr, St. Apatil!"

The guard who was in charge of the prison was amazed when he saw this great miracle. He went to St. Apatil and prostrated himself humbly and reverently before him. Kissing his feet and head, he implored him, "Holy Father, have mercy on me, for I am in great distress! My only daughter is pregnant and has arrived at the time of giving birth. She has now been in labor for seven days, but the infant is unable to be delivered from her womb. Many physicians, exorcists and magicians have been brought to her, but none have been able to help in the least. Have pity on me, and pray to your God for her. For I believe that if you do this she will be free from certain death!" Apatil replied to the guard, "Bring me a little oil. I shall prayer over it, and then take it to your daughter and anoint her with it. In this way the glory of my Lord Jesus Christ shall be manifested." And immediately the man took the requested oil to Apatil, and the saint prayed over it and made the sign of the cross upon it. And the guard took the oil back to his house and anointed his daughter. And immediately she delivered her baby without difficulty. The infant was a boy, whom she named Apatil, in honor of the saint whose prayers had saved her life and that of her son. And great indeed was the rejoicing in that house on account of this wondrous thing!

After this had happened, the fame of St. Apatil's miracles reached the ears of the governor. He was furious and perplexed about what he should do next. And suddenly the devil appeared before him, having assumed the form of a soldier. He said to him, "Listen to me, and I shall advise you wisely. I know all about this power which the Christians possess. Now what you should do is find a very beautiful woman of licentious morality, adorn her with every article of seduction, and place her into the prison with Apatil. She will be able to deceive him [and to lead him from his virtue, by means of the temptations of the flesh.]"

So the governor selected a woman who was very desirable in appearance and of licentious moral character. He had her dressed as a prostitute and adorned with jewelry and finery of the most beautiful kinds, and placed her in the same prison cell as Apatil. The governor felt confident that she would seduce the holy man, whose purity was such that the angels would have admired him. As soon as she entered the presence of the blessed man, he recognized for what purpose she was there, and prayed to the Lord, saying, "My Lord Jesus Christ, do not let the charity with which you have loved me be overcome!" The woman perceived the radiant grace of God which shone forth through the face of Apatil, and at once she fell to his feet and implored him to help her achieve salvation. Once Apatil had told her many things which pertained to obtaining salvation, she was filled with Heavenly desires. And when she departed from there, she made a vow to serve God alone and to cease from her former, sinful way of life. From then on she withdrew from society and lived as an anchorite, showing herself to be a Christian of the greatest fidelity. Indeed, the example of her conversion caused a great many others to be converted to the Faith, in humble fear of the Lord.

When the governor came to know of this, he ordered the saint to be led out of prison and brought into his presence. He said to him, "By the gods! O Apatil, I have worked very hard [to make you see your error, and so to save your life.] But you have failed yourself." The holy man replied, "Do not spare me anymore! Either put me to the sword or throw me to the beasts. And you shall come to know that none of these things are able to separate me from the love of my Lord Jesus Christ. To Him do I hasten to go, if I have been made ready to receive the eternal blessings which He has prepared for those who love Him."[78]

The wicked governor said to him arrogantly, "These 'eternal blessings' of which you speak are of no concern to me. With such talk you have deceived the crowds, so that they no longer acknowledge the official gods. It is these gods, not your, who keep us safe and bestow true life to all human beings, and nourish beautiful bounties as the reward of those who believe in them and venerate them! But I will ensure that, because of your flagrant ingratitude towards these blessed gods, your flesh shall be thrown as food to the beasts! Thus everyone shall come to know that they have been given life by the [Roman] gods. It is these gods who give fruitfulness to the soil of the earth, for the joy and consolation of humankind. But they remove from the face of the earth all fools like you, who refuse to give due thanks for their kindly gifts!"

---

78 Cf. 1 Corinthians 2:9.

The governor then ordered the saint to be bound with chains and his skin stripped from him from his head to his feet. Then, while he was drenched in his own blood, a hungry, nursing[79] lioness was to be released upon him, until nothing of his own flesh remained upon his body. [The saint was bound and flayed, as ordered.] When the lioness was brought in to him, she rushed at him furiously at first. But as she approached closer, she [became tame and merely] licked his wounds. When the governor saw that the lioness did not devour him, he commanded that the animal be removed. And how great was the outcry which was made at that time by all the crowds [when they learnt what had happened.] In wonder and awe, a great multitude gave forth abundant praise to God!

The governor turned to one of his trusted advisors and said to him, "What should we do with this wizard? He has spurned the glorious edict of the emperor and refuses to honor the gods. Instead he declares himself openly to be a Christian." The advisor replied, "My lord the governor, carry out upon him a sentence [of death], or he will end up deceiving everyone." The governor therefore issued the sentence of death. It read thus: "Because Apatil, a useless and ineffective soldier, resists the imperial edict and refuses to worship the gods, but rather declares himself to be a Christian, I order that his head be cut off, according to the imperial laws."

When the saint heard this sentence of death, he exulted in his spirit. It was then the seventh day of the month of Meshir.[80] Once he had been led to the place of execution, he asked the

---

79 Literally, "a lioness producing milk". Possibly this condition enhanced the animal's ferocity.

80 February 14. There seems to be an inconsistency with this date and the date given in the title of the work for his martyrdom (the sixteenth day of Epip, i.e. June 23). That later date will be give very shortly in the narrative as that on which his body was interred in its tomb. But it is also possible

soldiers who escorted him that they should permit him to pray first. They agreed, and so he turned his face to the east and prayed thus:

> *"I give thanks to you, Lord God, my Savior, for You have made me worthy to share in Your life-giving sufferings. You have bestowed upon me the chance to die for the sake of Your blessed Name. I beg You, O Lord, that You accept my spirit in peace, and not hold against me my failings and errors—either those of which I am aware or those of which I am unaware.*
>
> *May Your holy angels accompany me, lest the powers of darkness, which inhabit the air and which hasten always to do evil, should impede my journey to You. Lord God, you have permitted me to travel across the perilous ocean of life by Your constancy and strength, which you have bestowed upon me. Through this constancy and strength, I have confounded rulers and manifested the greatness of Your holy Name in the presence of governors.*
>
> *Grant to me now, my Master, that I may pass to the celestial realms in the sky without peril, and so may arrive at the door of Your heavenly charity without fear or obstacle. And thus may I come to hold to You, whom my soul loves, and to embrace You, who have bestowed upon me victory. There I shall*

---

that some time elapsed between the issuing of the sentence of death, and the saint's execution—although this is not indicated in the text.

receive from Your hands the imperishable crown of fidelity, and rejoice eternally with the company of Your holy martyrs.

For to You belongs the glory of all aeons, together with Your Heavenly Father and the Holy Spirit, the giver of life, both now and forever and through all eternity. Amen"

Once Apatil had pronounced the concluding "Amen" of this prayer, a voice from Heaven came to him, saying, "Come now, O beloved martyr of Christ, St. Apatil! Rest with all the souls of the saints, with whom you shall receive eternal blessings and peaceful tranquility in the Heavens, throughout ages which have no end." When he heard this Apatil again exulted in his spirit. He urged the soldiers to proceed, saying to them, "Please, do promptly that which was commanded to you." And he knelt down in silence and fearlessly stretched out his neck, awaiting his execution. One of the soldiers displayed to him the warrant containing the death sentence. Then, with a single blow from his sword, he cleanly struck off the holy man's head. And so Apatil departed from this life and went to Christ, whom he loved, to remain with Him for all eternity.

Now when the soldiers had all taken their leave from the site, a group of faithful men came and took away the body of St. Apatil. They clothed it in burial robes and buried him with all befitting honor and dignity. They placed his body in a tomb alongside the bodies of other holy martyrs, who had completed their struggle for the Faith before him.

After this Sotericus, the father of St. Apatil, heard that his son had been martyred. Both he and his other son, John, hastened to his place of burial. From there, they took his body back to his home province of Sabaru. The people of that province then experienced peaceful and prosperous times. They built for Apatil a most beautiful tomb and interred his body there on the sixteenth day of the month of Epip.[81] At that site, many great miracles and healings occurred, to the glory of the Holy Trinity, and to the honor of the blessed martyr of our Lord Jesus Christ. To Him be all glory, all honor and all adoration, together with his Heavenly Father and the life-giving and consubstantial Holy Spirit, both now and always and for all eternity. Amen.

May the blessing of St. Apatil be with you all! Amen.

And I, [the writer of the narrative,] sincerely repent for all my sins and failures. May you, [my readers,] remember this unworthy disciple [of the Lord], who am but dust and ashes, and may the merciful God have pity upon me. Amen.

---

81 July 23.

The Martyrdom of St. Lacaron of Tgeliensis

The Martyrdom of St. Lacaron, and those who died with him; who completed his glorious struggle [for the Faith] on the fourteenth day of the month of Paopi,[82] in the Peace of God. Amen.

I

It came to pass in the eighteenth year of the wicked emperor, Diocletian,[83] when Arius was governor of Antinoopolis,[84] that he boarded his yacht and began to sail to the south, until he arrived at the port of Siout. Taking his mount upon a beast, he entered the city seeking out Christians, in order that they should be forced to worship the impure idols [of the imperial authorities]. The governor sat himself in the city amphitheater, and commanded those who were present to bring before him all Christians of the city.

Once these had been led to him, he asked them, "Will you sacrifice to the gods of the emperor, or not?" With one voice they responded to him boldly, saying, "We shall never sacrifice to these impure, lifeless and abominable idols! We profess openly that we are Christians. Our God is in Heaven, and He shall be our helper." Then Arius the governor commanded to his troops that each of these Christians should be decapitated by the sword. And so they achieved their martyrdom, and their souls flew upward into Heaven in radiant glory.

After this had been done, a certain official approached the governor and told him, "My lord and governor, there is a certain

---

82 October 24.

83 C 302 AD.

84 Modern day Sheikh 'Ibada.

soldier here. Not only does he refuse to worship the imperial gods, but he tells others that they are not gods at all. He does not obey your orders, and has declared himself openly to be a Christian." Upon hearing this, the governor grew enraged, and ordered this soldier to be brought into his presence. Immediately the officer led the soldier in question into the presence of the governor. He then asked him, "What is your name?" The saint replied, "If you enquire of the name which my parents gave to me, it is Lacaron. This is my name according to the flesh. But my real name is 'One who is Called by Jesus Christ'." The governor continued, "And how old are you?" Lacaron answered that he was fourteen years old. The governor asked him his trade. To this Lacaron replied thus, "I am a solider, now fighting for a king who will eventually perish and die. But soon, I will be a solider fighting for a King who will never die, the King of kings, and Lord of lords,[85] my Lord Jesus Christ!"

The governor, much perplexed, asked him, "My son, why have you deserted your legion? Tell me where you have come from." St. Lacaron responded, "If you wish to know the truth, I am from Tgeliensis, from the legion stationed at Siout. But my desire is to be a soldier of the King of all Heaven and all earth, my Lord Jesus Christ, the monarch of all the ages! I have departed from my former legion, which shall soon be reduced to death and nothingness. I openly confess myself to be a Christian, and am proud to be counted amongst the followers of my Lord Jesus Christ, the Lord of Heaven!"

The governor said to him, "Offer sacrifice to the gods, and I will let you go free. You are a soldier—and yet you are being disloyal to your superiors, by declaring yourself to be a Christian! But we sincerely wish to show you mercy. If you simply make the required sacrifice, you shall be treated with all honor."

---

85 Cf. Revelation 19:16.

Lacaron answered him, "I pray that I may please the King of all, and so receive from Him a crown of immortality! Do not imagine, O governor, that I shall be led astray by your deceptive words. Because of my Faith in my Lord Jesus Christ, I despise you and all your empty words!"

Upon hearing this the governor was filled with wrath, and ordered his troops to throw Lacaron to the ground and have him scourged with a whip made of calf sinews, and firmly told to be obedient to the imperial commands. Lacaron spoke to him with gentle mercy, saying, "My command is that I should obey the laws of the great and true King, my Lord Jesus Christ, who saves all those who hope in Him."

The governor then ordered him to be flogged until his blood flowed forth onto the ground. He said to him, "Sacrifice to the gods, lest you come to a terrible death at my hands!" But Lacaron answered him, "O son of iniquity! God is our helper, and He is able to protect us and to save us from your hands. But you and all your wicked kings shall utterly perish."

At this, Arius commanded Lacaron to be suspended from a stake and to be tortured until his insides spilled onto the earth and his blood soaked his entire body. The just youth endured this torment with all fortitude and courage. Afterwards, the governor ordered him to be thrown into prison while he considered how to torture him next, for he was handsome in appearance.[86]

That night, as Lacaron lay in prison, the Lord appeared to him and said, "Be strong, Lacaron, my son, for I am the Lord Jesus

---

86 The significance of Lacaron's handsome appearance to the governor's consideration of how to torture him is ambiguous here. It may be that the governor felt some degree of hesitation to torture him, because of his good looks. On the other hand, it may be that the governor specifically wished to torture him in a way that would destroy his appearance (as some of the subsequent treatments suggest).

Christ! Conduct yourself manfully and take courage. I shall be with you in all the afflictions which you are to undergo. I swear to you by Myself, that you shall enjoy the eternal banquet with all my saints in the Heavenly Jerusalem. Your name shall be venerated in every land and your martyrdom shall be celebrated throughout all the earth. Be brave and take courage!" And then the Savior embraced him and granted to him His peace, before ascending into Heaven surrounded by His angels. Blessed Lacaron then spent the night in a vigil of prayer until the light of dawn arose. He was filled with Faith and confidence, which the Lord had bestowed upon him.

When morning had arrived, the governor Arius commanded that his tribunal of judgement be set up, and ordered that Lacaron be led before him so that he could judge his case. When the saint was led into his presence he chanted the psalms as he walked, singing, "O God, come to my aid and save me in Your name!"[87]

The governor then commanded that the saint be bound to a bed of iron, and his mouth to be held open with steel forceps. Then his teeth were to be extracted, one by one, and molten lead to be poured into his mouth and all over his body. After this horrible thing had been done, he directed that Lacaron should be suspended from a stake and cruelly scourged. While this was happening, the blessed martyr cried out continually, "My Lord Jesus Christ, free me from all of these harsh torments!"

But immediately the governor ordered the bronze bull[88] to be brought in, and Lacaron's body to be affixed to it with long nails and sharp needles. This was done, but the saint felt no pain whatsoever. The governor then ordered the bronze bull to be

---

87 Cf. Psalm 54:1.

88 This 'bronze bull' was a dreaded instrument of torture in the ancient world. Precisely how it worked in this context is not clear.

drawn by the machines attached to it, so that all of the limbs of the saint should be torn asunder, until his body should become like the dust of the earth. But blessed Lacaron endured all of this with incredible fortitude, [remaining quite unharmed.] Afterwards, the governor, [thwarted in his intention of torturing or killing Lacaron,] ordered him to be thrown in prison again, with his feet firmly bound in fetters of iron.

II

St. Lacaron's fame soon spread throughout the entire city, for it was obvious to all that he was a man of God and that the Lord was with him. Now, there was a certain woman in the city, whose son had been ploughing in a field with his oxen. One of these animals had collapsed and died immediately. When the woman heard about the miracles of St. Lacaron, she went to him in the prison, and implored his assistance, saying; "O [destined] martyr of Christ, I beg you to help me! For as my young son was ploughing the field today, one of his oxen fell to the ground, dead."

When Lacaron perceived the woman's humility and earnestness, he said to her; "Take this staff of mine. Place it over the body of the ox, and tell the beast to arise and stand up in the name of the Lord Jesus Christ. It is, indeed, for the sake of His holy Name that I have undergone all these tortures." The woman took the staff from Lacaron, and went and placed it over the head of the ox. She said to it, "In the Name of the Lord Jesus Christ, the God of St. Lacaron, arise and stand up alive!" And immediately it arose and stood up, fully alive. All the gathered crowd, when they perceived what had happened, gave glory and to God and praise to Lacaron.

There was also a man imprisoned with Lacaron who was possessed by a demon. He fell on his knees before the saint and said to him, "If you wish, you are able to heal me!"[89] The blessed youth said to him, "Do you really believe that my God is able to heal you?" The possessed man replied, "Certainly, I believe." And immediately the saint arose and prayed, saying, "O Jesus Christ, my Lord and my God, let it be done to this man according to his Faith!" And the man was immediately restored to perfect health from that moment onwards. And all who were in prison, when they saw what had been done, cried out joyfully, saying, "There is one God, the God of St. Lacaron, and none else apart from Him! And He hears all those who cry out to Him from their hearts."

And there was another man, a leader of the city, who had been incarcerated because of taxes which he owed to the civic authorities. When he saw what had been done, he arose and kissed the feet of St. Lacaron and begged for his help, saying; "I implore you, O servant of God, that you administer to me the sacrament of Christian baptism!" Lacaron, perceiving that he genuinely held the true Faith, made the sign of the cross upon the ground with a finger of his right hand. And immediately there flowed from the ground a stream of pure water, with which he baptized the man in the holy Name of the Father, the Son and the Holy Spirit.

There was a woman held in the prison, too, who was afflicted by a demon. This demon threw her to the ground, and cried out, saying, "I beg you, holy Lacaron, do not torture me! I shall leave this woman of my own free will. I am a dog-headed demon in my form, and for fourteen years I have inhabited this woman, who has become my dwelling place. But now, I shall go out from her."

---

89 Matthew 8:12.

Lacaron said to all of those who were in the prison with him, "Let us arise and pray". He stood up, and with hands extended, prayed thus:

> *"My Lord Jesus Christ, hear my prayer and accept my pleadings! Behold the tears which I pour out.*
>
> *Each of us knows you to be the God who raise up the humble, and the helper of those to whom there is no other helper.*
>
> *It is You who stretched out Your blessed Heavens and made them stand firm. You adorned them with the brilliant ornament of the stars. You are the one who weigh mountains on scales, and place the rivers on a balance.[90]*
>
> *You appeared in the womb of the immaculate Virgin Mary, so that You might save the entire human race from perdition. You showed yourself to Your blessed apostles, so that they might preach Your most holy Name, in order that You should be praised and that Your immense, blessed and radiant goodness should be glorified throughout the whole world.*
>
> *Glory to You, my Lord Jesus Christ, forever and ever! Amen."*

Once Lacaron had said "Amen", all of those in the prison responded "Amen!" Immediately the demon threw the woman to the ground, and, in the likeness of a great flame of fire, flew

---

90 Isaiah 40:28.

out of her. And all of those present acclaimed, "There is one God, who is the God of St. Lacaron, and none other besides Him!"

Again, there was another man, whose arm had been cut off. He went to Lacaron, and begged for his help, saying, "Please help me, sir, for I am suffering greatly." The blessed youth held forth his finger and made the sign of the cross over him, saying; "Place [the stump of] your [severed] hand into your armpit, and, in the great Name of Christ, you shall be healed." When the man had placed [the stump of his arm] into his armpit, he drew it forth again, and it was restored, just like his other hand! When the crowd who were held in the prison witnessed the miracle which had been performed they were utterly amazed and cried out together, "Truly, there is no God on Heaven or Earth, except for Jesus Christ, the God of St. Lacaron!"

When Arius the governor heard of all these wonders and miracles which Lacaron was performing, he commanded him to be led before him at his judgement seat. The governor said to him, "You should know that I have done my best to be able to spare your life until now." But the saint answered him, "Please, do not spare my life any longer!" As he spoke, his face shone with radiant brilliance like the sun. But the governor persisted, "Make sacrifice, O Lacaron, or you shall die a dreadful death." The saint replied, "Yesterday, you have spared my life. Today, spare it no longer! I am ready to die for my Lord Jesus Christ, and I shall offer to Him my body as a sacrifice. Indeed, it is written, 'Fear not those who can kill the body, but are not able to kill the soul'. [91]"

Upon hearing this, the governor ordered him once again to be suspended from a stake and be scourged, until his intestines spilled out from his abdomen. But while this was happening, the

91 Matthew 10:28.

blessed saint raised his eyes to Heaven, and prayed, "Hear me, my Lord Jesus Christ! Send forth your holy archangel Michael, that he may assist me in this my hour of need."

And at once the archangel Michael appeared from Heaven! And he collected the intestines of the saint which had spilled out, and restored them to his abdomen. He freed him from the stake from which he was suspended, so that Lacaron was now at liberty and completely free of any wound or visible damage to his body. And when the torturers saw the angel, which had restored his spilt innards, they were all filled with wonder and believed in God.

All of the torturers then removed their official belts of military service from around their waists, and threw them to the ground before the governor. They spoke boldly, saying to him, "We openly confess that we are now all Christians! We are now joined to all those who believe in the God worshipped by St. Lacaron." Upon hearing this, Arius was filled with fury and was perplexed and confused by their actions and declaration. "What have you witnessed to make you say this?" he asked them.

They answered him, saying, "What we have seen and witnessed we are not able to communicate to you. Indeed, it is written, 'Do not cast your pearls before swine, lest they trample you with their feet, and turn upon you and destroy you'.[92]"

Flaring up in furious anger, Arius the governor responded, "You miserable wretches! Do you not realize that your bodies are entirely within the power of my hands?" But the torturers, [now converted to the Christian Faith], said to him, "Do to us whatever pleases you! We are not able to be vexed by your tortures, because God is with us, and He will help us." He then ordered that a great pit be dug, and an immense fire be lit within

---

92 Matthew 7:6.

it. The blessed men who had been converted threw themselves into the flames willingly. And thus they nobly completed their martyrdoms and received an imperishable crown. [Having died for their Faith in Christ, their souls] ascended to the Heavens in glory.

One of the governor's advisors said to him, "My lord, if you let the prisoner Lacaron remain within the city, everyone here will come to believe in him. He has worked great wonders through the name of this Jesus, who has been the cause of anger and anxiety to kings throughout the world!" Meanwhile, blessed Lacaron, in whose mouth the grace of God shone radiantly, continued to sing the psalms unceasingly; "Lord, do not be silent from my praise, for the mouths of the wicked boast against me."[93] And when he had completed his prayers with an "Amen", he fell asleep and rested peacefully.

---

93 Psalm 109:1-2.

III

In the middle of the night, St. Lacaron arose. He prayed once more, saying, "Lord, open my lips and my mouth shall declare Your praise."[94] And he continued, "In the middle of the night, I shall arise and praise the righteousness of Your judgements."[95] When the holy youth had completed these prayers, the wicked and cunning devil assumed the appearance of an angel of God. Thus disguised, he appeared before the saint and said to him, "You have made many prayers before God, and He has sent me to you to comfort you. When you appear before the governor tomorrow, you are to answer whatever he asks you [with mild compliance and] without any indignation in your heart. In this way, you shall gain for yourself [the favor of] the God of Heaven.

But blessed Lacaron recognized this apparition to be the devil in disguised form. He said to him, "Depart from me, Satan, you minister of evil! For you have no part with the servants of Christ, the Son of the living God!" Upon hearing the name of Christ, the devil at once took on the appearance of a blazing flame of fire, and disappeared hastily. And blessed Lacaron said

---

94   Psalm 50:15.
95   Psalm 119:62.

in his heart, "Let us be wakeful and pray, lest my enemy the devil should deceive me."

Now the governor, when he sat at his tribunal of judgement, ordered Lacaron to be brought before him. Once he was there, the governor addressed him thus, "I do not require that you should sacrifice as I [and other the officials] do. All I ask is that you burn a little incense upon the altar of the gods. And then I shall let you go free, and you shall escape any torture." But the blessed man responded to the governor, "You are trying to seduce me from my Faith with your gentle words! Truly, these words and sentiments provoke God and His holy angels to justified anger."

Then the governor, [inflamed with black rage,] ordered a bench to be brought in and Lacaron to be placed upon it. He commanded that long nails be brought forth, and these be driven through the saint's body. One nail was to be driven into his right side and another into his left side, until they came out the other side and fixed him to the stool. Then a nail was to be driven through his head, until it came out through his groin. And thus the saint was affixed to the stool. And the governor said to him [sarcastically and mockingly], "Lacaron, may the God in whom you have placed your faith come to you and save you from my hands, that I may witness his power!"

And behold! An angel of the Lord suddenly appeared from Heaven. He removed all the nails from the body of the saint, and thrust them into the body of the governor! And the governor cried out [in pain], saying, "Lacaron, now I know that your God, whom you worship, is truly powerful! If He heals me from this pain, then I shall certainly believe in Him."

But Lacaron answered him, "I know that you will never really believe, [and that your words are deceptive.] But for the sake of the crowd who are present here, I shall pray to my God. It is for

His holy Name that I have endured these tortures at your hands, yet He, in return, shall grant to you healing." Then Lacaron raised his hands over the governor's body and prayed thus; "My Lord Jesus Christ, whom I adore, show Your power, so that all this multitude gathered here may know that You alone are God and that there is none other than You. And, doing this, they shall come to praise Your holy Name!"

Once he had uttered this prayer, the nails softened to become like water, and fell out of the governor's body onto the ground. Once this was done, the governor [arrogantly and stubbornly] responded, "Truly there is no god who is like Apollo or Artemis! And it is through the power of these deities that I have been healed." To this Lacaron responded, saying, "You should know that you are still within my hands, [since it was my prayers to the Christian God which healed you]!"

The governor was infuriated and said to his torturers, "Bring to me many instruments of punishment and place them before this wretch! Then I shall have him tortured, so that he shall see clearly that his God is not able to save him from my hands." When these vast array of instruments of torture had been brought, the torturers attempted to punish Lacaron with them. Yet not one of them was able to affect him at all. They did not cease torturing him from morning until dusk, yet he remained completely unmoved and unafflicted by any of their attempts.

The governor was overcome by wrath when he witnessed this. He arose and seized one of the weapons of torment, and attempted to strike Lacaron on the head with it. But it slipped out of his hand, and flew violently at his own head! And the governor's head was severely wounded. At this, blessed Lacaron laughed and said, "Indeed, the psalm of David was not lying when it said, 'Those who fight against me will be humiliated and shall fall',[96] and 'Their own swords shall devour them, and their arrows shall be broken!'[97]"

The governor replied to him, "I declare through the power of the Romans and through the great god Apollo, Lacaron is a wicked worker of wizardry!" He ordered his tortures to bring forth a great wheel of wood, and said to him, "Throw this wretch under it, so that his body is cut in half!"

And when the saint lay under this great wheel he began to suffer immensely, for his body was, indeed, being sliced into two pieces. At this point, the holy martyr raised his eyes to Heaven and prayed earnestly;

> *"Hear my prayer, O Lord, and do not be silent to me! For I am a stranger and a pilgrim like all my ancestors.*[98]
>
> *Do not abandon me, O Lord, the God of my strength. Do not allow me to die, until I have confounded this wicked wretch. Grant to me the fortitude to endure this torture for the sake of Your holy Name, so that I may find eternal favor in Your sight.*
>
> *O Lord and God of the whole universe, the merciful and compassionate, count me amongst the sheep of Your flock. And grant to me strength, through Your own most radiant and boundless power!"*

96　Psalm 27:2.

97　Psalm 37:15

98　Psalm 39:12.

Once he had said this—behold!—our Lord appeared before him and said, "Be strong, my blessed martyr and beloved of my Father! Come to me, so that I may show you your glorious crown. After you return to the tribunal of judgement, you shall fight for My Name and you shall indeed confound this wicked governor!" Then the Savior immediately took him upwards to His glorious Heaven and revealed to him its celestial splendors. He embraced him with all the saints, and showed him the wonderful throne prepared for him, together with the crown and robe of immortal glory. And all the noble saints there blessed Lacaron with one voice, and said to him; "Be strong, O holy martyr and courageous athlete of Christ your King! You shall certainly gain the glorious inheritance of the Kingdom of Heaven!"

After the Lord had shown him all these marvelous things, he returned his soul to the world below, where his body was still positioned under the weight of the heavy wheel. He then took Lacaron's limbs, which were being torn asunder, and fashioned them together once more and restored him to perfect soundness so that there was not the slightest trace of injury upon him. And the Lord said to him, "Peace be with you! Go forth, and confound this godless governor in the sight of all this crowd!"

After this Lacaron arose, [completely unharmed,] in full view of the governor and the assembled onlookers. The impious governor, [feigning that he did not recognize the youth], said to him, "I do not know who you are! Get away from here, you scoundrel!" Lacaron responded, "Why do you pretend you don't recognize me? Am I not the one whom you ordered to be cut into two? But my Lord Jesus Christ came to me. He took my severed members and joined them together once more and restored me to perfect well-being, [as you can see.] And He has sent me back to you, so that I may confound you and all your wicked rulers!"

Then all the multitude of onlookers who were present cried out in wonder, "The God of St. Lacaron is the one God, and there is no other besides Him! His name shall endure for ever and ever." But the governor said to the crowd, "Do not become unduly excited! All of these things are mere works of wizardry. Let us ask him for another sign and if he is able to do that, then perhaps we shall believe in his God."

Then the saint extended his hands, and prayed;

> *"O God, You have created Heaven and earth and all that is contained therein. You sent Your only-begotten Son into the world, who gave to us His own Body and Blood to redeem us from our sins.*

> *Receive my prayer this day. Show Your power in the presence of this tyrant and of the crowd which is around me, so that Your holy Name may be glorified and all this multitude may know that there is no God except for You, the Lord God Almighty, and Your only-begotten Son and the Holy Spirit, forever and ever. Amen."*

When he had said this prayer, the sandals which were on the feet of the governor were transformed into a living calf! This happened in the presence of the governor and all the crowd. But the governor, [exasperated], said to the people, "Did I not tell you that this Lacaron performs magical tricks!" He immediately commanded the calf to be slaughtered and its flesh thrown to the dogs. Then he ordered a surgeon to be brought to him, and Lacaron's tongue to be cut out. When the surgeon had arrived, [Arius] said to him, "Take this youth, and amputate his tongue, because I cannot bear to listen to all his words!"

Once his tongue had been cut out, [miraculously] Lacaron again spoke to the governor. "You have cut out my tongue," he said, "so that I wouldn't be able to speak to you. But now I have taken up a tongue of the spirit, against which you and your father, the devil,[99] have no power."

[Having overcome his surprise,] the governor said to him, "Listen to me carefully! Taste the food which has been placed upon the altars [of our gods], and drink the wine that has been offered in sacrifice. [If you do this simple thing,] I shall let you go free and you shall escape all further tortures." But blessed Lacaron replied, "God forbid that I should ever do this! Indeed, it is written, 'You are not able to eat both from the table of the Lord and from the table of demons'.[100]" The governor burned with wrath, and commanded the saint's mouth to be forcibly opened, and the flesh that had been offered to idols to be brought in and forced into his mouth.

When all these things had been done to him, the governor said, "Lacaron, leave behind this foolish faith which you place in your God!" But the saint answered, "Your joy [and triumph] is not yet complete, you enemy of God and friend of demons, you who are a stranger to all the ways of the blessed!" Then the infuriated governor had him cast into prison once again.

---

99 Cf. John 8:44.
100 Cf. 1 Corinthians 10:21.

IV

When the next morning had arisen, Arius the governor commanded Lacaron to be brought before him once again at his tribunal of judgement. St. Lacaron wondered to himself in his heart, "What will this godless wretch do to me next?"

Once he was before the tribunal, the governor addressed him thus, "Sacrifice to the gods, O Lacaron, or you shall die a most dreadful death at my hands!" The blessed youth answered him in a gentle voice, and said, "I shall not sacrifice. Do to me as you please. God is with me, and He is my helper. He is like a tower of immovable rock surrounding my body and my soul." The governor answered, "O Lacaron, by these words you force me to torture you all the more severely. But simply offer sacrifice and I shall let you go free!"

But the saint now held his silence. Then the governor continued, "If you wish for me to give you a few days, during which you may carefully consider your actions and situation, please let me know, [and I shall do it]." But the blessed youth answered, "Before I came to you now, I have already carefully reflected with myself. So do as you please to me! My body may be in your power but my soul and my spirit belong to my Lord Jesus Christ."

When the governor heard these words from St. Lacaron, he commanded that he should be suspended by his head from a column for three days. The governor's soldiers did as they were directed. Lacaron, while suspended from the column, prayed thus; "My Lord Jesus Christ, first and greatest of martyrs, who rule all the ages by Your Divine power, send to me Your holy angel to bring me assistance!" Once he had said this, behold, an angel of the Lord appeared above him, and released him from the column and placed him safely upon the ground, without any harm at all. And the angel encouraged him, "Have courage and be strong, O athlete of Christ, for the conclusion of your struggle is drawing nigh." Having spoken thus, the angel of the Lord embraced him and then ascended upwards into the Heavens, while the saint looked on.

When the third day had arrived, the governor ordered his troops to go and see whether Lacaron remained alive or whether he was dead. The soldiers who had hung the saint from the column went to see if he was still alive. And they found Lacaron [calmly] standing under the column, [free and unharmed.] At this, they were astonished and cried out, "We are now all Christians, we proclaim openly! Let us be counted amongst those who believe in the God who has saved Lacaron!"

And they removed their belts of military service, and went to the governor and threw them in his face. The governor, [bewildered,] said to them, "What is it that you have seen that makes you cast away your belts of official service and place your faith in the God of Lacaron?" The soldiers replied to him, "What we have seen we are not able to explain to you, for you are now as a stranger and alien to us." The governor exclaimed, "O you perverse and foolish knaves! I have spoken in a kindly manner to you, and you have spoken in this wicked way to me. Yet I do not know what sentence I should impose upon you, since you have not been baptized yet [and are therefore not yet, technically, Christians]."

When blessed Lacaron, the athlete of Christ, heard the governor saying all of this, he said to the soldiers, "Take courage, because my Lord Jesus Christ is with you!" And then he prayed, saying, "My Lord, look upon me and these, my brothers, for they now stand with me and glorify Your name." And St. Lacaron made the sign of the cross above the ground, and there immediately gushed forth a spring of sparkling water, like [melted] snow. He baptized them all forthwith, in the name of the Father, the Son and the Holy Spirit.

The soldiers all then said to the governor, "Behold! God has made us worthy to receive His baptism, as you have seen with your own eyes. Pass whatever sentence you like on us, so that we may leave you." Upon seeing and hearing all this, Arius was enraged and commanded that each of the newly-baptized soldiers' heads be cut off with a sword. And immediately his executioners proceeded to decapitate them all. And thus, on the twentieth day of the month of Thout,[101] they completed their battle [for the Faith], each one receiving an imperishable crown in the Heavens.

After all these things, Arius, the governor, turned again to St. Lacaron and said to him, "Make sacrifice to the gods! Surely, you do not wish to die a terrible death at my hands, for I know that you are wise." The saint responded, "I am indeed wise if at all times I seek the Kingdom of my King, the Lord Jesus Christ. To this Kingdom I shall soon go and receive there the prize of an immortal crown." Hearing this, the governor ground his teeth in fury, and said to him, "Oh! Since you will not obey me when I instruct you to do what the Emperor has commanded, I order that your head be taken off with the sword!"

---

101 September 30.

When the blessed youth heard this sentence, he gave thanks to God. Then the executioners placed a bridle on his mouth and led him to the place of execution. He requested of the executioners, "Please allow me a little time to offer prayer to my God." And a great multitude of onlookers had gathered around. St. Lacaron raised his hands and prayed, saying, "My Lord Jesus Christ, stand with me today! Give me fortitude until I have completed this battle."

And immediately the Savior Jesus appeared before him—none other than the one Holy Lord in whom he believed. And the saint said to the Savior, "My Lord and my God, you have indeed heard me when I prayed to you! Now, my Lord, I beseech You to grant that for which I ask, for You are merciful and full of compassion." To this, the Savior responded, "Whatever you wish, I shall grant for you!"

Blessed Lacaron continued;

> *"My Lord, I ask that you do not permit my body to be corrupted in the earth, but that you preserve it, and that a shrine be built over it.*
>
> *And to whomsoever shall build this shrine over my body, grant a reward for their labors in the Heavenly Jerusalem and number them amongst the multitude of Your blessed. And if anyone makes a vow over my tomb and fulfills it, may You bless him and all his house.*
>
> *My Lord, do not allow any fierce gale nor any wild beast to enter my tomb. Do not allow any filthy adulterers or any impure spirit to approach the place where my body is buried.*

If anyone afflicted with illness or besieged by a demon comes to my tomb and venerates my body, grant to them healing and wellness.

And to all those who write down the story of my martyrdom, let the sentence due to them for their sins be erased, free them from the evil snares of the devil, and may Your blessing, mercy and peace remain with them and their entire households.

Those who undertake efforts and labors to make pilgrimage to my tomb, and there respectfully venerate my body, pour out upon them Your mercy, bless them and forgive them their sins.

O Lord, to me also, though a wretched sinner, grant tranquil rest upon account of Your great mercy, O God, lover of the human race, who bestow generous rewards on all who believe in You! Amen."

When Lacaron had concluded these words, the Savior spoke to him, "Act with courage, for all your struggles will come to an end very soon. I swear to you by My own self that I shall fulfil all that I have promised to you, and shall even do things for you which exceed that which you have asked. I shall place my angels as guardians over your body both day and night, who will receive the prayers of all coming to your tomb. They will communicate these prayers to me and I shall bless all those who have offered them according to their merits." When he had said these things, the Savior embraced him and then flew upwards into the Heavens.

The saint then spoke to the executioners and said to them, "Come and complete the task you have been assigned!" As the executioners approached him, blessed Lacaron stretched out his neck, and they beheaded him. He thus completed his heroic witness to the Faith on the fourteenth day of the month of Paopi.[102] And an immense light shone in that place, and a sweet fragrance enveloped it, from the multitude of angels which came to receive the soul of St. Lacaron. And the Savior Himself took his soul up to Heaven with these blessed angels, who followed his ascent. The entire choir of the Heavenly host came to meet them and embraced the martyr, before taking his soul to the celestial city of our Lord, God and Savior, Jesus Christ. To Him be all glory, together with the eternal and gracious Father, and the life-giving Holy Spirit, forever and ever. Amen.

---

102 October 24.

www.ingramcontent.com/pod-product-compliance
Lightning Source LLC
Chambersburg PA
CBHW022130080426
42734CB00006B/293